A GLOBAL LESSON

ALSO BY REINHARD MOHN

Success Through Partnership

Humanity Wins

An Age of New Possibilities

A GLOBAL LESSON

*Success Through
Cooperation and
Compassionate Leadership*

REINHARD MOHN

WITH Andrea Stoll
TRANSLATED FROM THE GERMAN BY Helga Schier

C. Bertelsmann

CROWN PUBLISHERS
NEW YORK

Translation copyright © 2009 by Crown Publishers, a division of Random House, Inc.

All rights reserved.
Published in the United States by Crown Publishers, an imprint of the Crown Publishing Group, a division of Random House, Inc., New York. www.crownpublishing.com

Crown is a trademark and the Crown colophon is a registered trademark of Random House, Inc.

Originally published in German in Germany as *Von der Welt lernen: Efolg durch Menschlichkeit und Freiheit* by Verlagsgruppe Random House GmbH, München, in 2008. Copyright © 2008 by C. Bertelsmann Verlag, München.

Library of Congress Cataloging-in-Publication Data is available upon request.

ISBN 978-0-307-58768-8

Printed in the United States of America

Design by Level C

10 9 8 7 6 5 4 3 2 1

First American Edition

*This book is dedicated to my wife, Liz Mohn.
I am grateful for her tireless commitment to
the objectives of our corporation and
for our companionship in our journey through life.*

Special thanks to my assistant Susanne Knetsch. Her judicious preparation and continued support have greatly helped create this book.

CONTENTS

FAMILY ORIGINS AND PERSONAL LESSONS

EXPERIENCES OF AN ENTREPRENEUR

ON THE ROAD INTO THE FUTURE

A GLOBAL LESSON

FAMILY ORIGINS AND PERSONAL LESSONS

ABOUT THIS BOOK

To this day I still enjoy my daily hour-long walks through the forest. I need these moments of solitude. Having time to think without interruption gives me strength and relaxes me. This has helped me in many situations throughout my life. Where am I? What are my next steps? Are my goals realistic? What could I do better? These are the questions that have accompanied me over the decades. They are inextricably intertwined with my journey through life and with the creation of the Bertelsmann Corporation.

I was born in 1921 in Gütersloh, Germany. The turbulent twentieth century presented me with innumerable challenges, and often I wasn't sure how to handle them. When I returned from the war as a young man in January 1946,

I never would have dreamt that from the rubble of the destroyed publishing house would grow a media company with offices in more than fifty countries and with more than one hundred thousand employees. How the conditions in our society have changed since then! The political and cultural changes of the past five decades have initiated a process of globalization, challenging the way we think and do things in our daily lives. This process even influences the development of democracy in Germany.

Throughout all those years the Bertelsmann Corporation has had the opportunity to collect manifold experiences, developing its enterprise in shifting political climates in Germany and Europe, as well as in the United States, Russia, India, and China. Considering the challenges of globalization, these experiences seem more relevant than ever. How were we able to establish a dialogue with people of such different origins and beliefs? What entrepreneurial decisions were necessary to successfully manage an international company with more than one hundred daughter companies? Why did Bertelsmann in Germany during my time never see a labor strike? In short: What is the secret of our success? In spite of many setbacks and unavoidable disappointments, I say: It was worth it.

And if today, at the end of my long journey, I'd be allowed one wish, it would be this: Peeking into the future, I would wish that the tried and tested Bertelsmann management style might provide the foundation of a peaceful coexistence of cultures.

All over the world, people tend to cling to habits as if they were eternal and to chain themselves to well-established traditions. Fear of what is new, a resistance toward what is other, toward what is different, has always promoted prejudice and dogma, which have historically found the most significant realization in national states and political systems. But the Greek philosophers already knew that the real challenge of life is to accept the process of constant change, *panta rhei*.[1]

History has shown time and again that power and violence cannot uphold any given human world order eternally. This experience is still relevant today. What is it that enables us not only to endure, but also to view the incessant changes in the cultural, political, economic, and national realm as an opportunity to build the future with personal strength and independent action? And what intellectual, political, economic, and social conditions are necessary for success?

These are the questions I have explored over the decades. Looking back on my own personal and entrepreneurial experiences, I now want to reveal the motives that guided my development.

PROTESTANT TRADITIONS AND MY DESIRE FOR INDEPENDENCE

As far as I can remember, I've always been fascinated with the freedom of one's own thinking. As a sixteen-year-old student whose homework assignment was to discuss "My

Thoughts on Choosing a Profession," I was able (much to my surprise today) to single out three aspects: a sense of responsibility toward society, one's natural abilities, and the desire for independence and a meaningful life.[2] What was important to my future then has not lost any significance today.

My upbringing in a disciplined and strict religious household may have played an important role. It provided a frame of reference for my character development, which required an early sense of responsibility and self-discipline. At the same time, my upbringing fostered my spirit of opposition and encouraged my search for my natural abilities and inner motivations, which my Christian education alone could not satisfy.

Anyone growing up with four older siblings and one younger brother is no stranger to the joys and hardships of human society. In my parents' house, my brother Hans Heinrich played the part of the most respected and loved firstborn. But the part of the youngest remained uncast for five years, until my brother Gerd was born, because a girl who had been born after me did not survive. The sound of the church bells at her funeral is one of my earliest memories.

I was considered a sensitive child. I had inherited my father's predisposition for allergies and was somewhat susceptible to colds. But being ill also meant being alone. My mother Agnes's strict household did not allow special treatment. I clearly was the fifth wheel in our large family, carefully watching the rituals of our family's life and my older siblings' activities without feeling like a participant. If there was something I didn't understand, I rebelled inside and would sometimes withdraw. This was bound to lead to conflicts in a household governed by Christian principles and strict discipline.

As the publisher of Bertelsmann, my father often hosted lunches with authors and business partners at our home to discuss matters of the publishing house. Children had to keep quiet, of course, which was sometimes difficult for me and didn't always make sense. As punishment, my mother would often have me "stand in the corner." After a while, she'd ask me if I was ready to behave. No!, I'd declare (to the amusement of my siblings), I didn't want that at all!, and the whole ordeal would start all over again.

My mother, Agnes, was the daughter of Pastor Seippel of Gütersloh. Due to her mother's early death, she had had to take on the responsibility for her younger siblings. The result was a strong belief in discipline and an uncompromising sense of duty, qualities that she passed on to her own children. With loving stringency, she administered our education in a huge household, which included servants, houseguests (school friends of one of my older sibling's), as well as official guests of my father's. When I was young, my grandfather Johannes Mohn and my grandmother Friedericke, née Bertelsmann, were also part of that household. Both sides of the family lived close by, and we were tightly knit. My sisters graduated from the all-girls high school, while my oldest brother and I attended the Protestant High

School in Gütersloh. Even so, we didn't really go to school *together;* I had just started sixth grade as he was graduating high school, with straight A's.

The great age difference among us siblings led to other experiences. My parents would regularly travel to Switzerland or the Black Forest with my four older siblings, while I was sent to church camps. I didn't understand that at the time. From one day to the next I was left behind, alone among strangers, and, young as I was, I had to rely on myself. This experience was my early training in being alone. But what was painful for the child was a challenge to the youth: Why was this happening to me? Did I agree with it? What would I do differently, what would I do better? If you are suddenly without your family or any sympathetic ear, you learn to engage in conversation with yourself. And you learn that your own thoughts may lead you further than what is brought to you from the outside. Being alone as a child has taught me to talk to, and listen to, myself. And I still do so, to this day.

The traditions of our Protestant publishing house, which had been in family hands since its foundation in 1825 and had been managed by my parents, Heinrich and Agnes Mohn, since 1921, the year I was born, permeated our family's life. My grandparents' stories would bring to life historical anecdotes of the publishing house. Over and over again they'd make us aware of the historical origins of the publishing house founded by the Protestant lithographer Carl Bertelsmann in 1835. His many experiences as church council leader and city official, providing both a religious and an entrepreneurial model to his son Heinrich, were a natural part of our family conversations at the dinner table. My grandfather Johannes Mohn, too, had been active as city official, Presbyterian church master, and curator of the Protestant High School in Gütersloh (cofounded by Carl Bertelsmann). And he had been director of the board of many missionary societies, as well as a board member of the Association of Protestant Book Dealers. All that in addition to his leadership at the publishing house. A Protestant conviction and lived entrepreneurship was as natural to my siblings and me as our daily bread. Through prayers at the table and worship at our home, during which my father would read from his prayer book and accompany the hymns on the piano, our Christian education permeated our private lives. And, of course, church attendance on Sundays was mandatory!

My father's personal leadership style followed in the Protestant tradition established by Bertelsmann's founder, Carl Bertelsmann. In the first half of the twentieth century, the lithographic company had developed to a midsize publishing house, which, after World War I, in 1923, shrunk to only six employees from eighty in 1910. In the wake of an increasing openness to popular literature, the publishing house grew to four hundred and forty employees by 1939. Despite this enormous growth, the company's management style lost none of its patriarchal character: mutual loyalty and compassionate concern were still an undiminished priority. Following the Christian tradition, nobody was to work on a Sunday. My grandmother made sure of this with the threat of cutting off the electricity! Following the family's tradition, the sense of personal responsibility taken by the Bertelsmann publishing house toward its employees extended even to social initiatives. For example, my grandparents and parents were concerned about the betterment of their hometown, so they initiated the foundation of a preschool (in addition to other social initiatives). And, for the benefit of their employees, they established a pension and company health plan.

These various activities, along with the fluctuations of the company's business during the economically unstable 1920s, were an additional burden on my father's high-strung sensibilities, already strained by his asthma. Although we were children, we were quite aware of the terrible unemployment and the suffering of so many people after World War I; not only was this the subject of many conversations, but our own family's sometimes meager meals became unforgettable memories of my generation.

Due to my father's asthma, the family moved to the healthier climate of Braunlage in the Harz mountains in 1923. This is where I started school. But staying in the low mountain range only brought temporary relief for my father's condition, so we moved back to Gütersloh. My father's health declined steadily during the 1930s, and at the start of World War II, he was practically unable to work.

My father had very little impact on me personally; by

and large he passed on only a few helpful insights. Without a doubt, the formative personality in my childhood was my mother. If I had problems at school, I talked them over with her. My hay fever, which plagued me from day one all my school years, along with my stress-induced fevers and my dyslexia (undetected at the time), took a high toll on my classroom performance. Consequently, my mother had doubts about my talents and abilities. Eventually I transferred to the branch of our high school that focused on the natural sciences. It was then that I discovered how much I enjoyed sports. My health improved, as did my performance at school. But the fears and insecurities of early years would still echo inside me. As a senior I didn't have the confidence to assume the office of class president offered to me by my classmates. But in 1939 I did graduate as one of the better students.

There is one incident in particular that sticks out from those years, which illustrates my early reflections on personal responsibility. One day we had a spelling test. At the end of the class the teacher collected the notebooks and handed them to me, since I, as the elected student liaison, held the key to the teacher's desk. During the break, one of the students came up to me, saying he had made a mistake on the test, and that I should give him his notebook so he could correct it. His request created quite a dilemma for me. I was torn between my feelings of friendship and my sense of responsibility.

Despite deep reservations, my feelings of friendship won

out, and I honored my fellow student's request. That night I couldn't sleep! As soon as morning came, I confessed my mistake to my mother. She discussed the situation with my oldest brother, Hans Heinrich. That same morning, Hans spoke to the principal, who came to the conclusion that giving the key to a ten-year-old student had not been a wise decision.

This experience stayed with me for a long time. I learned one of my life's lessons, and have since avoided difficult situations with improprieties!

Without a doubt, I was a child with an active inner life, a child who thought long and hard about experiences at home and at school. Above and beyond my technical and mathematical interests and talents, I was searching for a deeper meaning. The religious discipline of my parents' home, however, with its daily rituals of worship and prayer, did not offer me true motivation. More memorable by far were the religious teachings of Pastor Florin. His teachings were different because he didn't only want to pass on the well-known themes and contents of the Christian faith; he also wanted to make the biblical stories relevant to us. This, for example, is how he described the Sermon on the Mount: Jesus told his disciples that he'd give a sermon on a nearby mountain. His disciples informed the believers, adding that the endeavor might take a while longer, and that it might be advisable to bring along provisions. And after Jesus had spoken on the mountain for several hours, his disciples reminded him to announce a break for bread, because people were hungry. Jesus followed their advice and broke in half two large pieces of bread the disciples had brought along, letting them distribute it. Everyone in the audience unpacked their own provisions and thus everyone had enough to eat. This vivid and realistic interpretation of a miracle impressed me greatly—told like that, religion was suspenseful and convincing!

My parents, on the other hand, noticed more and more that a purely formal education in religious matters meant little to me. The older I became, the less formal religion touched me. After my confirmation, my mother left it up to me to decide whether I wanted to participate in the family's worship. This had been a long time coming, and I decided to no longer participate.

Because of the large size of our family with its divergent interests, a most important question became ever clearer to me, until I couldn't avoid it any longer: "Who am I? Which way shall I turn?"

MY YOUTH DURING NATIONAL SOCIALISM AND WORLD WAR II

By Easter 1939, when I finally held my diploma in hand, freely choosing a profession was already out of the question. Following my technical inclinations, I had intended to undertake the study of engineering after completing my six months' civil service (required of all males of my generation). But Hitler's march into Poland on September 1, 1939, put an end to this plan once and for all.

National Socialism had molded the private and social life of the 1930s to conform to its ideology. Therefore my youth, as well as that of my siblings, was tightly controlled by our membership in NS-youth organizations: the Jungvolk, the Hitler-Jugend, and the Bund Deutscher Mädel. But I felt that my parents were politically guarded.

With my support, an independent group of historians conducted a detailed historical reappraisal of the history of the Bertelsmann publishing house in the years between 1933 and 1945.[3] Here I'd like to stay true to my personal memories, aligning my retrospective assessment of those years with my personal experiences.

My Protestant father focused his publishing vision on works of theological content. Due to his health problems, he had to delegate many tasks to his executive employees.

The inflation after World War I brought Bertelsmann to the brink of financial ruin. Of the eighty-four employees on our payroll in 1921, the year of my birth, only six remained two years later. The publishing house had to survive, and my father supported the measures suggested by the management in the 1920s to diversify the publishing program to increase revenue. Little by little, popular literature made its way onto the publishing list. This ensured our survival in the midst of a worldwide economic crisis. Fritz Wixforth, then director of distribution, undertook an initiative that aimed for widespread impact: popular literature in high volume and at low prices. This, along with special window displays in retail bookstores, made spectacular sales possible.

Before long, this distribution model influenced the traveling sales and mail-order book business. Combining thematically linked books in one set allowed traveling salesmen direct sales. The use of such sets had played an impressive role even prior to World War II. We understood, for the first time, that the retail book business, however well organized, did not cover all markets in our country.[4] The fiction and poetry collections in so-called field-post editions also generated great commercial successes for the publishing house.

There is no doubt that during the Third Reich, Bertelsmann applied these business models to further the development of the publishing house. Yet I did not sense any personal political involvement of my parents above and beyond what was necessary to ensure the interests of the publishing house. Yet anyone who, like my siblings and me, had absorbed the ideals of a national community as taught in National Socialist schools, youth organizations, and sports clubs, would, even as adults, march with excitement and without hesitation toward the abyss that led to the outbreak of World War II.

The catastrophic consequences of an entire nation's blindness came to our door only days after the war had begun: My oldest brother, Hans Heinrich, was killed on September 10, 1939, in Poland. My mother suffered from this to the day she died. Her oldest son had been the apple of her eye, the desired heir, the future of the family. After his death, she would spend a lot of time alone in his room, which was to be preserved as it was during his lifetime. Hans Heinrich's death changed the life of the entire family. My mother, who had always been a very active woman, began more and more to live in the past.

I had to make my own decisions in the fall of 1939. I was a proven track and field athlete and glider pilot. I adored flying. If you volunteered for the service, not only were you favored for an officer's career, you were also allowed to choose your arm of service. I was hoping for a career as a pilot and started my service in an air and field training command in Quedlinburg. By January 1940, I was transferred to an airfield command, and shortly thereafter to the air defense. After several months of duty at the Western front, I was admitted to the officer's training near Utrecht. One year later, in January 1941, I was promoted to second lieutenant. But despite my proven fitness to fly, my dreams of becoming a pilot would never materialize. Instead, the leadership qualities I had developed in early years drove me to ever-more challenging situations, both personally and materially.

As a twenty-one-year-old officer, not only was I in charge of four air defense guns and rapid-fire cannons, but I also had forty-five previously convicted soldiers under my command. This was in the Netherlands.

This would have been a challenge even for a seasoned officer. For a man as young as I, dealing with a group of crafty, violence-prone men was rather risky.

When one of the soldiers asked for weekend leave, I agreed. Regular leave was his right. "That's okay," I said, "but please remember that you have to be back on time! You know what happens if you are not. I am required to notify my superiors, and as a previously convicted soldier, this will result in a transfer to a penal colony." It was clear to us all that transfer to a penal colony sealed the fate of any soldier. My orders were clear. But as the evening of his return progressed, the man was not back at the appointed time. I can still see myself standing high up on a railway bridge, considering what to do. Finally I went to sleep. About an hour later, the man knocked at my door, which was guarded by a soldier. "Let's compare time," I said to the man, "I have exactly twenty-four hundred hours." "Yes," he responded. "Lieutenant, will you report me?" I replied, "I do not want to discuss this with you now. We will talk about what needs to be done in the morning." But the man knew I had no choice but to follow the rules to the letter and to report the incident. One exception would have made me vulnerable to blackmail by these men, and I would have been at their mercy.

Only a little bit later, at around two in the morning, the soldier standing guard over the weapons called me. "Lieutenant," he said, "the man shot himself." I got up, got dressed, and strapped on my gun. It was a bright, moonlit night. I walked over to the soldiers' quarters. They could all see me. I didn't know what to expect. It was a difficult situation. The man was lying dead in the recreation room, a suicide note full of anger and vengeance next to him: "I am taking Mohn with me to the happy hunting-grounds," it said. Of course, the news spread like wildfire.

I reported the incident to my superiors immediately. A court-martial was unavoidable. The incident was investigated in all details. The court-martial questioned not only me, but everyone else as well. The noncommissioned officers had to justify themselves, and there wasn't a single one among them who had anything negative to say about me. Finally the court-martial criticized the commander and declared: "You've made a mistake. You don't give such a difficult task to an officer as young as this one."

Despite the positive evaluation, this incident was one I could not shake off. I questioned my youthful behavior again and again. I know that based on who I was at that time and in that place, I could not have dealt with it in any other way. I have always walked the straight and narrow in my life. In fact, there were times when striving to do right was my only guidance through difficult situations. For during the years in the German army, I had to master other difficult situations.

I was transferred to the Göring Regiment in Berlin and had the opportunity to witness the grotesque figure of the Reich Marshall up close, face gaudily made up. I wanted to be transferred to the front as soon as possible, just to get away from this environment and to be relieved of guarding Göring's hunting castle, Carinhall. The commander in charge of me was surprised by my request but understood.

I was transferred to the reserves of the Göring Regiment in France. There, too, I had to make difficult, far-reaching decisions that made me, young as I was, reflect upon leadership styles. Throughout my youth I had experienced nothing but the hierarchical leadership style of National Socialism, and no doubt I had internalized the demands of discipline and obedience. But I had to learn that hierarchy and discipline were not always enough. You cannot easily persuade people until you are willing to understand the individual and his motives. Leaders lead by example!

I was neither ready nor able to see the abyss into which the NS ideology and its murderous war had pushed us. But I began to have my own thoughts. My observations of the behavior of the Nazi leadership in general (and some officers in particular) posed unanswerable questions to me. In the fall of 1942, following Rommel's last offensive in El Alamein, our regiment was militarized and transferred to Italy. But once the Americans landed in March and April of 1943, we were transferred from Naples to Tunis in order to face the American and English forces on African soil. It took only about two more months before another fate was decided, this time in the mountains of Mateur near Tunis.

That morning my scouting patrol and I were in the process of climbing a mountain. We had heard that the Americans were approaching from the other side. We had to be extremely careful. In order to get a view from the top of the mountain a few hundred yards ahead, three soldiers and I crawled through brush and thorns. As soon as we had seen the tanks, I was shot in my right leg. I knew I could not return. Therefore, I ordered my patrol to retreat as quickly as possible, before any of us could be seen, even though it meant leaving me behind. My comrades carried the news of the approaching Americans to our post, and I waited to see what would happen to me.

But then an American soldier appeared. Neither of us knew quite how we could communicate. In the American's eyes, I was the personification of the evil German. I spoke little English. But I tried to point out my wound and gesticulated that I needed his support if we wanted to leave this place together. We looked at each other, sizing each other up. He could have shot me. After all, the situation was risky for him, too. He'd only be certain if I really was incapacitated once we'd descend the mountain.

In this very tense situation, we both decided to trust each other. We approached each other, the stranger, the enemy, as human beings. This experience had a great impact upon me. The decency of this man has been an example of humanity to me—one that I would summon up in many difficult situations to come.

Supported by the arm of this unknown soldier, I stumbled toward a hospital administered by the British. Only a few days later the Afrika Korps made up of German and Italian soldiers surrendered, and hundreds of soldiers, myself among them, began the journey into British and American captivity.

MY TIME AS A POW AS AN OPPORTUNITY

After half a year in a North African camp, I was shipped to the United States, as were many other soldiers. I would spend the next two years in a prisoner of war camp in Kansas. Camp Concordia, which was considered an officers' camp, held four to five thousand soldiers. Upon my arrival I didn't know that the Pentagon had set up Concordia as a model camp for the ideological reeducation of Germans. Nor did I know that the years in Kansas would be among the most important years of my life.

Unlike most of my fellow soldiers, I was accustomed to being alone from my earliest childhood days. I was able to lose myself in thought on walks or in private moments in my room. I was enthusiastic about the camp library and also took advantage of the opportunity to borrow books from the University of Kansas and to watch movies. Camp Concordia had its own university, which was supposed to further educate its prisoners. I eagerly studied English. The outbreak of World War II had cut off my chance to go to university. But then and there, from behind the barbed wire of an American prison camp, I could gaze upon the world. It was there in Concordia that I first learned about the German concentration camps. Faced with that, which seemed so incomprehensible, the ideals of my youth shattered.

To a young man who had spent nearly his entire youth under the banner of National Socialism, Concordia provided a second chance. Now I was eager to know everything: What had happened in Germany? Why had my entire generation succumbed to National Socialism? Although it was strictly forbidden, I would listen to German military reports on the shortwave radio, while learning through the free press how events in Germany and Europe were viewed in the USA. Speeches presented different topics, and discussions afterward gave us the opportunity to explore these topics from various points of view. But it was Captain Strong's personality that made a lasting impact on me. His striving to always do right, along with the great respect he showed his prisoners, have remained an ideal within my memory. It was there, in the American prison camp Concordia, that I learned for the first time what democracy really meant.

In general, camaraderie, fairness, and discipline were strong among the soldiers in the camp. But I also noted that the self-discipline and sense of responsibility decreased as the rank of the officers increased. Clearly, this was food for thought.

The preparation courses for engineers held at the camp's university were most interesting to me. I had not yet given up on my dream. At the university, I met a young man, Rudolf Wendorff, who, like me, had fought in Africa, and who was active on the camp newspaper. He wanted to interview me for an article, and so he dropped by my quarters. There I was, in a self-made rocking chair, lost in thought. The young man was impressed. We became friends, met for sports activities, and had many discussions on our daily walks through the camp.

As prescribed by the camp leadership, prisoners had to

do labor service. I worked on about thirty different farms in the states all over the Midwest. I found myself face-to-face with the self-assured, self-reliant attitude of the Americans. If there were problems, they faced them head-on. People would roll up their sleeves and help one another without too much concern for rules and regulations. When lasting rainfall flooded the tents of the prisoners, and our camp's guards did not want to deal with it, the people of the nearby town lent a helping hand. "This is a culture, a society I can live in and support," I thought. This type of community, which truly distinguishes America, and which I have seen time and again in later years, goes back to the first settlers' fight for survival. Influenced by the American pioneer spirit, people do not wait for the administration in Washington, D.C., to help. First they look for ways to help themselves.

If it had been up to me, I would have stayed in America at the time. But the Geneva Convention was very clear: At the end of the war all POWs, without exception, were to return to their home countries.

In the fall of 1945, I was shipped back to Europe only to spend another six months in a French POW camp. These months were very depressing and took a toll on my health. But my time in America had taught me to respect other people's perspectives, and so I could now understand the French attitude after the war.

In winter 1946, the time finally came. Many prisoners rolled back into Germany aboard freight trains. I found shelter in a release camp near my Westphalian home.

THE BERTELSMANN EMPLOYEES
EXPECT THAT I TAKE LEADERSHIP

What I saw when I arrived in Gütersloh in January 1946 was shocking. Seven weeks before the German capitulation, air raids had reduced my hometown to rubble. Large parts of the Bertelsmann building were destroyed, and little was left of the production lines.

The printing press was burnt out, as was the paper warehouse that had stored half-completed books, galleys, and rough prints. My parents' house had been seized by the British. I hadn't been aware of any of that. Along with the breakdown of inner conviction came the nearly complete destruction of the outside. We didn't know how to go on. Once again I found myself in a situation where I had to put aside my personal aspirations. After having attended many technical lectures at the camp's university in Concordia, I had carried hopes that I'd be able to start my engineering studies after all. But once back in Germany, my parents immediately made it very clear that they had different expectations. Hans Heinrich had been killed; my second oldest brother, Sigbert, was missing in action in Russia; and my youngest brother, Gerd, was only twenty years old and too young to take on the responsibility for our publishing house.

My father's health left no doubt that he was no longer capable of managing the publishing house, either. What to do? I asked for two days to think it over. I did what I had always done in difficult situations: I went to the outskirts of town and wandered the forests and fields close by. I needed solitude.

On my walks through the ruins of our town I recalled what our driver, Henke, had said upon my arrival: "It is good that someone from the family is back!" Clearly this resonated with many of the town's citizens. Approximately one hundred people had stayed with Bertelsmann and met among the ruins every day. They sorted through the rubble, figuring out which machinery was still in working order. Of course, they also hoped for food. And I joined them.

In those first few weeks, we fought our way through the desolation, the cold, and the poverty. It became clear to me, day after day, how many hopes rested on my shoulders. I could not turn my back on this responsibility. Soon I had to face the quandary of how to rebuild the publishing house. I had learned how to manage people even in difficult situations during the war years. I had also learned that personal motivation was vital. People can endure extraordinary hardships and achieve a great deal if they feel that their personal goals are the same as those of the group at large. If the individual can identify with the objectives of the group, anything is possible. And I knew that in order to have credibility in these situations, you had to set an example.

We faced enormous difficulties. Our director of distribution managed to get a large supply of paper from the Netherlands so that we could start up a number of the functioning printing presses. But other than that, we lacked just about everything that was necessary for regular production. We improvised to reclaim the production halls. We didn't even wait for a building permit. Finding the necessary coal supply was an adventure—often I had to appeal to the employees' sense of community to ensure that what we managed to collect did not fall victim to private redistribution practices.

Our biggest challenge by far was getting a printing license. My father was ill, and our old management—led by Gerhard Steinsieck, Gustav Dessin, and Theodor Berthoud—was no longer acceptable to the British military administration. It was only the resignation of these three leaders on February 27, 1946, that finally opened the doors. Approximately one month later, Bertelsmann received its license to publish. Meanwhile Rudolf Wendorff, with whom I had become acquainted during my time in the American prison camp, had come to Gütersloh to manage our editorial department.

Thanks to the efforts of all our employees, rebuilding the publishing house proceeded in leaps and bounds so that by summer 1946 we had a definite increase in production. But our difficulties with the British occupying administration were far from over. New license applications meant new complications. I recall having many conversations with the British licensing board during that spring, 1947.[5]

In my meetings with Padget-Brown, the officer in charge, it became quite clear that the British were willing to give more wiggle room to a politically innocent young man than to my father, who bore the history of the publishing house during the Hitler years. Therefore, in April 1947, my father transferred the direction of the two publishing houses, Carl Bertelsmann and Der Rufer, to me, retroactive from January 1, 1947. This situation was a huge burden to me, yet at the same time it was an incredible opportunity. I was determined to use it well!

I was twenty-five years old at the time. I knew that I lacked an important ingredient for fulfilling my new role as the leader of a publishing house: I had never had any training in the book business. But my experiences in the war and as a POW had taught me many things that are never taught in business school. I had learned self-reliance. And I knew how to persuade people, how to excite them. Without individual commitment to the goals of our community, the difficult tasks awaiting us could not and would not be handled. My experiences with the NS dictatorship and its demise, along with the efficiency of the Americans I had witnessed, convinced me that the patriarchal management style practiced by generations preceding me was no longer applicable. I wanted to lead in a new way!

APPRENTICESHIP AND INITIAL STEPS
TOWARD A NEW CORPORATE CULTURE

In a speech on New Year's Eve 1946, I appealed to our employees to build the foundation for our future livelihoods in a spirit of "mutual trust and courage."[6] I made it clear that upcoming improvements in our production methods would not only serve the company's bottom line but also be advantageous to each and every employee. I was only following my personal convictions in this matter, but in doing so I had unwittingly laid the foundation for our corporate culture, albeit without really understanding where this might lead. By balancing individual and corporate interests, I had taken a step toward the model of cooperation, a model I would further develop in the decades to come.

In the summer of 1947, I learned the basics of the book business at the book-dealer school in Cologne-Marienbronn, and then at the university bookstore Calvör in Göttingen. In my studies I had the opportunity to test my newfound self-assurance and my entrepreneurial spirit, which had been roused by this personal challenge. All students in Cologne had to take a three-hour final exam. Hard as I tried, the single exam question eluded me. Weeks later we received our corrected exams. The teacher was obviously worried, for the exam results had been awful. There was a single exception to the terrible results. Reinhard Mohn had been the only student to explain why the question could not be answered. The instructor conceded that he had given us a question that was *impossible* to answer. His courage impressed me.

During my apprenticeship in Göttingen, I found myself facing problems familiar to me from my work in Gütersloh. Improvisation was necessary here, too, for there were shortages everywhere. Almost every day Dr. Richter, the manager of the university bookstore, sent away customers who were looking for some scientific book or other they needed for their work. How this man would have liked to fulfill their wishes! Alas, there was no paper for new editions. But I quickly discovered that the nearby paper factory (*Feldmühle*) would exchange new paper for waste paper: two pounds of new for four pounds of waste. My boss was impressed. So I made a sign and put it in the window: ONE NEW BOOK FOR TWO POUNDS OF WASTE PAPER. By the time I left Göttingen, the profits of the Calvör bookstore were up.

Our ability to improvise was helpful in Gütersloh as well. But it was first and foremost the wealth of ideas and experiences that our distribution manager Fritz Wixforth came with that saw us through the first few years after the war. Wixforth had been at my father's side since the 1920s, developing new distribution models constantly. To me, he was an indispensable teacher.

I got to know the qualities of this man on many trips and company visits. Wixforth was not only a good judge of character, he also had ample charisma, inspiring customers and business partners alike. Nothing was beneath him in those difficult years at the beginning. He would work the trowel as hard as the telephone, and he proved himself a master of bartering who could get us coal in exchange for liquor, or clean bookbinder linen in exchange for potatoes. But most important, the booksellers remembered him. Fritz Wixforth and Bertelsmann were met with trust everywhere.

Thanks to the paper supply that Fritz Wixforth had found in the Netherlands, production in Gütersloh slowly picked up. As early as 1946, we were able to pay a regular salary to more than two hundred employees. But no matter how hard we tried, the lack of spare parts, coal, and paper brought production to a standstill more than once. It wasn't until the currency reform on June 21, 1948 (which effectively terminated the black market), that conditions stabilized. In the fall of 1948 and during the following Christmas season, we sold virtually all our inventory. Much to our surprise, people wanted to buy books, because there wasn't much else to buy yet. The German customers were thrilled to be able to get anything at all for their money.

Our successful Christmas sales seemed to confirm that our publishing business was on the right track. We increased our publishing list to the extent our upstart production line would allow it. In order to encourage the booksellers, who had been hit hard during the war years, Fritz Wixforth decided to reinstitute a former distribution model from before the war: The bookseller was not billed until the end of the year, and also had the right to return unsold merchandise. So, in 1949, we shipped most merchandise with a return guarantee, hoping that customers would react as positively to our product as they had at Christmastime.

But times had changed; the currency reform had altered the conditions of trade and the range of goods for sale in the Federal Republic of Germany. The display windows were full again; it was not surprising that those who had suffered during the war needed things other than literature: building materials, food, clothing, shoes, stockings. The Christmas season in 1949 was a near catastrophe for Bertelsmann. In early 1950, our return guarantee required that the publishing house take back an unseemly large amount of books. Our financial reserves were exhausted. In this situation we had to ask ourselves whether Germans were really as disinterested in literature as the disastrous holiday season of 1949 seemed to suggest. Perhaps there were other reasons for the lack of success. We made two decisions: The return guarantee was not sustainable in its current form. And we refused to accept that the low Christmas sales were indicative of the consumer disinterest in our product.[7]

Bertelsmann's survival was at stake in 1950. The situation forced us to look at other distribution models. Our prewar success with traveling salesmen and the mail-order business led us to reestablish relations with traveling book sales companies in the spring of 1950, which in turn led to the decision to try to reach new customers via direct sales.

OUR "KING'S IDEA" AND THE TROUBLES OF THE ECONOMIC MIRACLE

We racked our brains and came up with and discarded many different models. Of course, we discussed the distribution of sets. We also thought of selling books by subscription, hoping that it would lead to higher sales numbers, generating adequate commissions for the sales force.

The idea of selling books by subscription was not entirely

new. Book clubs had existed in Germany for decades, as the history of the German Book Club respectably shows. But these book clubs had not yet made use of direct sales. This is where we innovated. We structured the Bertelsmann book program so that it could be offered by subscription and sold door-to-door by a sales force. There were no models for this distribution technique. Therefore, the negotiations between our distribution department and our partners in the traveling sales and mail-order business were somewhat difficult and took several months. None of us knew the figures involved in a book club, but being the good mathematician that I was, I developed a formula specifically for our distribution model. We were ready to test the waters!

The model initiated by Fritz Wixforth, and which I put on fiscally sound legs, would become the "King's Idea" that paved the way for Bertelsmann's breakthrough.

On May 31, 1950, the Bertelsmann publishing house informed all German booksellers in writing that on June 1 Bertelsmann would initiate a "reading circle." Little did we know that this was the start of what would eventually become the largest book club in the world! The Bertelsmann publishing house would supply the publishing list and the marketing. The booksellers had to recruit subscribers and deliver the books. The business conditions were clearly defined: For a monthly fee each subscriber would receive two books per quarter. The booksellers would deliver the books, handle payment, and settle with Bertelsmann.

This two-step model offered advantages to both the bookseller and the publisher. It circumvented the natural competition between booksellers and book clubs that, unlike ours, were directly and exclusively linked to a publisher. The interface between the two steps was made possible by the discounts already typical between publishers and booksellers. Thanks to our high sales, we were able to offer cheaper prices than in a regular bookstore. This also gave us the opportunity to reach less affluent and less educated segments of the population, people who might hesitate to shop at a retail bookstore, for fear they might feel lost among the vast and varied selections of books.

The concept was a success from the start. Giving the responsibility for finding subscribers to the booksellers activated a wide net of distribution, mobilizing the economic potential of thousands of companies. No book club in the world had developed with such momentum! This model, however, which spawned such a rapid increase in turnover, also brought with it unimaginable risks and unforeseen challenges.

The evolution of the reading circle into a book club was defined by years of learning and the ongoing development of new and different solutions to overcome each new obstacle. For example, even in the first few months of the reading circle it became evident that the idea of selling each book at the same price (an idea that was convincing, originally) was untenable. The customers tended to choose the works with the higher production value. We had miscalculated. We immediately had to differentiate prices and incorporate additional payments.

Shortly after digesting this experience, we had to face an unprecedented rise in paper cost. This was the spring of 1951. We realized that we had miscalculated yet again, and that such high paper costs would surely drive the publishing house toward financial ruin. By that time the booksellers had already enlisted nearly one hundred thousand subscribers. The marketing successes were fantastic. Fritz Wixforth and his distribution partners urged us not to stifle this process with an increase in monthly fees. But our business practices had to be reconciled with our fiscal necessities. In long and difficult conferences, we were finally able to hammer out a 20 percent fee increase. What we feared—a marketing collapse and the subsequent loss of subscribers—did not materialize. The amazing popularity of the subscription book club had been confirmed.

By the end of 1950, the reading circle had two hundred and fifty thousand members, compared with the one hundred thousand registered readers we had had a year after its inception. By the end of 1954, we had one million members! But these successes had their downside. The unprecedented success in marketing led to financial problems that seem unimaginable in today's corporate world. For quite a while Bertelsmann's turnover doubled every year. Managing advertising costs, cash flow, and necessary reinvestments was nearly impossible with the available means and our rather humble profits at the time. In the midst of its successes, Bertelsmann had to stop, or at the very least drastically reduce, advertising due to cash-flow problems. The booksellers distributing our product naturally viewed this as a hurdle to their own interests and looked for alternative solutions. Several made deals with other book club companies.

This was a painful situation for me and the Bertelsmann management. My entrepreneurial days were full of sleepless nights, vacations cut short, and rather colorful odysseys to the banks. I needed to convince them that in order to grow we needed to invest. The pressure was immense. There were no known models for our plan, no known models for our attempts to react to unpredictable events in innovative ways.

At the time of the currency reform, when productivity was low, Bertelsmann had virtually no capital. Furthermore, the high taxation granted by allied laws did not support any capital building that was worth mentioning. While the reading circles reached their planned return, the ensuing profits were not nearly high enough to finance our fast expansion and necessary marketing investments. Inactive advertising expenditures were a burden to the profit balance.

While the banks registered the turnover increase of the Bertelsmann Company, they considered the lack of profit an indication of a lack of seriousness. In the eyes of the banks, our balance lacked noticeable assets. The value of the subscription base, which, by its very nature, had agreed

to continue purchasing our merchandise, was deemed not
credible enough to potential financiers. Bertelsmann had virtually no way to get credit.

Eventually, the method of draft financing offered a solu-
tion. The distributors paid their responsibilities with drafts,
which the publishing house would give out in turn as redis-
counts. For many years this is how Bertelsmann handled
its expansion. Everyone involved (especially the banks)
understood the inherent risks. There were so many nights
that I couldn't sleep. At the time I was only able to keep my
strength with relaxation techniques taken from the practice
of self-hypnosis.

I was constantly trying to think about alternative ways
to finance our enterprise. My situation often seemed to re-
semble that of Goethe's student magician, who can barely
control the masses of water he released. Our situation was
often rather adventurous. During the tempestuous times
of the economic miracle, Bertelsmann often operated at the
brink of insolvency.[8]

In the end, only our unwavering conviction and, later, our
certitude that, as per our own calculations, we would make
a profit, could justify these entrepreneurial maneuvers. This
method of financing worked only because the product of the
reading circle convinced its customers.

In order to better appreciate the financial risks we took,
one must remember that the budgetary tools and growth
calculations typical today did not exist at the time. Our only
compass was debit calculations and sales traditions. Busi-

nesses at the time lived hand-to-mouth, always teetering at the brink of disaster. Careful financial planning and medium-term fiscal politics were not applicable. If growth was just too fast, you simply had to hit the brakes. Luckily, the good relationships between Bertelsmann and its partners in the book business and shipping industry, as well as with the banks, made it possible to find a way out of many a "hopeless" situation. No bank in Germany today would finance such a high-risk enterprise. But even then we reached the limit of what many credit institutions were willing to support. I had to find different ways to finance our operation.

Once again my capacity for thinking outside the box came in handy. There was a rumor among our employees that Reinhard Mohn would take his Christmas vacation only to return on January 2 a new man. There is some truth to that. During the tempestuous times when I was building the company, I needed more than ever time to think. In order to get away from the incredible high taxation in the 1950s, my colleagues and I developed a model that would allow us to earmark as profit participation the monies that Bertelsmann otherwise would have to pay in taxes. My then two thousand six hundred employees would receive profit shares—with one condition: They had to lend this money to the company with 2 percent interest. This model coincided well with my understanding of cooperation and profit sharing. Both parties had advantages. An old diary entry by Rudolf Wendorff verifies that I had been thinking about the possibility of profit sharing as early as 1946.[9]

We tested this first model of profit sharing from 1951 to 1954, and then, due to changing tax laws, modified it to a company pension program. Our employees were happy with the equity growing in their accounts. And as for myself, the profit-sharing model had given me a path-breaking social tool that would give me food for thought in the decades to come.

EXPERIENCES OF AN ENTREPRENEUR

THE BUILDING BLOCKS OF OUR CORPORATE CULTURE

In every spare moment, on innumerable walks in and around Gütersloh, I would think about ways to reconcile the challenges of responsible corporate management with the conditions of dynamic corporate expansion. On cold winter days, I was often wrapped up in rather adventurous ways, but the people living in Gütersloh were accustomed to seeing Reinhard Mohn as a long-distance runner.[1] Considering our steady corporate growth, the traditional centralized management style at Bertelsmann seemed absurd. Clearly, under these conditions, corporate management would not be able to micromanage the onslaught of problems, let alone attack them creatively. Early on I had learned that neither the current group of managers nor I personally could possibly bear responsibility for further corporate expansion. If Bertelsmann was to grow even more, I had to delegate!

This process was difficult and painful. The second corporate level, which had yet to make independent decisions, was barely able to handle the new responsibilities. Our reorganization required training, constant communication flow, and painstaking personnel development. We hoped for the success; there were no guarantees. Only many years later would it become evident that these investments were the decisive foundation for Bertelsmann's success as well as its corporate continuity.

My experiences during the war and during reconstruction convinced me that the principles of fairness and compassion were the foundation of our corporate community. Time and again during these difficult startup years I was reminded that success hinged upon responsible leadership that takes into account the concerns of its corporate employees. Good employees are motivated employees! Handling these early postwar years had also shown me that treating employees as partners fosters creativity, the indispensable key for corporate success. We had to hold on to this sense of creativity!

Although I never studied business management, my work as publisher of a fast-growing corporation provided a perspective for the future. The tempestuous years of the economic miracle were a time of change and new beginnings. I understood that, to ensure success, one must face an unpredictable future with motivation, creativity, and the desire to help employees relate to the corporate objectives.

Starting in 1952, we expanded our line of reference books, securing the market share of Bertelsmann's dictionary division. In order to handle all of this, we had to update our printing techniques. In 1956, we introduced offset printing. That same year, Bertelsmann moved into the record business by founding the Schallplattenring (Record Ring). In 1958, we started the record company Ariola and the printing press Sonopress. Each one of these steps was an entrepreneurial challenge, and I had to rethink the organizational structure such expansions brought about.[2] Where did we stand? What could we do better? In all such considerations, my decision to delegate responsibilities hit the mark. Only with the cooperation of creative minds, who took the independence I had granted them as a great opportunity, would continued growth of the midsize Bertelsmann publishing company be possible. The communications with my employees became a forward-looking management tool. Innumerable conversations confirmed that only those who can relate to a company's objectives would take responsibility for that company's goals. In fact, the sense of relatedness to the company turned out to be an indispensable performance criterion. The willingness of employees to make independent decisions, and thereby further the development of their company, would only lead to success if they shared the goals of the corporate community.

As an entrepreneur, I was constantly envisioning strategies to create such a corporate community, and I began to lay the foundation for a corporate culture. Such a culture was indispensable in my interactions with my employees.[3] Many ideas came about in the close collaboration within our corporate community (which at the time was still defined by actual and direct contact with our employees). While my generation, which spent its youth in the war, worked hard during the years of reconstruction, we, corporate management and employees, also celebrated together with as much joy and enthusiasm. The company parties at Bertelsmann were legendary! The openness of the corporate interaction sharpened my senses for the hopes and dreams of the people I was responsible for, as well as for their needs as employees of a fast-growing company.

Even so, there were quite a number of confrontations between management and the union. At one point the management requested a lockout. This became a key experience for me! My image of humanity/compassion had been formed by the war and Germany's breakdown, but mostly by the way we all stuck together during the reconstruction of Bertelsmann. Therefore, it was impossible for me to fire the same people who had helped me sort through the rubble, just because of an irreconcilable conflict of interests. So I engaged in a direct dialogue with the workers' council, declining future membership in the management coalition.[4] Nevertheless, Bertelsmann was willing to accept the master wage agreement and to negotiate with the workers' council.

I had made this decision based on my personal convictions. In later decades, this would prove to be an outlook for a corporate culture based on partnership and cooperation.

The ongoing dialogue between corporate management and the workers' council is one of our most important achievements. Out of all of the experiences of the postwar years, it was actually the cooperation with our employees and their resulting motivation that proved to be the real engine of our corporate success. This notion of human partnership seemed to me the best way into the future.

In the year 1969, Bertelsmann looked back on 125 years of corporate history. How corporate behavior had changed in those years! And yet there was a consistency of corporate ethics, which my family had embodied in exemplary fashion. I wanted to adjust this to the times. I was aware that individual willingness to take responsibility could not be separated from corporate willingness to take responsibility toward the community. Personally, I felt that the religious teachings my parents had practiced and passed on to me were no longer applicable. I was looking for answers that would accept people as individuals and bring them back into the community as individuals. In my work as an entrepreneur, I wanted to anchor our corporate interaction in socially just company structures. My personal ideals of compassion and social responsibility were not just lip service.

My goal was clear, but the ways to reach that goal required a lot of time to think—time I didn't always have. Yet again, my natural inclination to seek solitude out in nature helped. In those days I would take twenty-mile walks in the forest near my Westphalian home nearly every weekend. On these walks I had the leisure to think through the questions the workweek had posed without interruption. It is there that I began to define the basic ideas for a corporate constitution, which would become a blueprint for the German corporate culture. In 1960, we introduced these thoughts to the public and presented the "Bertelsmann Constitution" at our 125-year anniversary. Following my inner convictions, I had prefaced our corporate constitution with the following ethical ideals: "The center of all our corporate considerations is the human being. The first and most important task of any corporation is to serve the individual. Therefore we evaluate our work based on the value it has for our fellow man."[5]

We "define justice and mutual respect, responsibility towards the company, leadership, personal initiative, forward-thinking planning, opportunities for career advancement and the relationship of work and compensation" to be the basic foundations of partnership and cooperation.[6]

Another important element was my own entrepreneurial responsibility to only make "use of the company's profits privately within a justified and justifiable compensation for my performance" and to be sure that as the "owner of the capital" I'd act in the interests of the company, while also fulfilling "my obligations towards society."[7]

This was by no means typical at the time, and unfortunately it still isn't today. But it is precisely these ethical considerations that are intrinsic to what I consider the example that entrepreneurial responsibility must set. Without setting such an example, social fairness within a corporation is impossible. I was optimistic that this new corporate constitution would help both our outward expansion and our internal corporate development.

A GLOBAL LESSON

In the years prior to World War I, Bertelsmann had established relatively few relationships with other countries, whether in Europe or elsewhere in the world. I wanted to change that! Influenced by my positive experiences in the American POW camp, it was my personal desire to become familiar with all large markets. As early as the 1950s, I went on extensive educational and business travels throughout Europe and the United States. It was clear that soon we would reach the limits of the German market, and so I began to look for markets outside of Germany.

The reading circle had managed to reach a new type of customer within Germany. Those who had never stepped inside a bookstore became avid readers through participation in our reading circles. By 1960, we had more than two and a half million members! After the tempestuous development years, the 1960s were a time to maintain our customer base and to refine our working methods. A new generation of managers took on this task, and the "reading circle product" would improve visibly. A marketing shift toward written advertisements and friendship marketing not only maintained our customer base but increased it even though we faced growing restrictions with our direct sales force. We had become the market leader in Germany. Our economic stability now allowed us to consider expanding into foreign markets. But before we could actually begin, there was much thinking to be done in order to establish new and preliminary contacts, and in order to undertake the necessary market research.

In the 1950s and 1960s, I traveled all over the world, examining cultural conditions and production situations. I was convinced that it was necessary to cooperate with local publishers in order to include enough product of local interest in our publishing list. The proven method of direct sales could function as a framework for mobilizing new readers even overseas.

One of my carefully prepared educational journeys in 1957 took me to Moscow.[8] I wanted to get information on the economic and cultural development in the Soviet Union, and so I flew from Hanover to East Berlin, and there took the train to Warsaw and finally Moscow. As had become my habit, I kept a travel journal to record my impressions.[9]

What caught my eye immediately was the juxtaposition between the magnificent boulevards and impressive historical buildings and the low living standards of the population. My visits at the Iswestija Publisher in Moscow, the model printer Zhdanov, and the publishing house of Pravda allowed me a glimpse of the reality of planned economy. Despite the occasional fantastic performance, the combination of a lack of competition, a strictly bureaucratic administration, often unfriendly working conditions, and the complete lack of social institutions left no doubt how wide the gap of economic development between East and West had grown. The joy of life so noticeable in the years after the war in Europe was completely absent in the Russian capital. And so I noted: "Moscow terribly fixed!"[10] But as far as social matters were concerned, I was impressed by the strength of the political system and the belief in the country's revolutionary achievements that shone through in so many discussions.

As publisher, I was impressed mostly by the numerous bookstores in downtown Moscow. I walked through the streets of the Russian capital, amazed. I had only a cursory knowledge of the contemporary Soviet literature, yet the familiar classics had set the bar high. A country with that many wonderful and sophisticated literary minds gave hope for literary development. The personal conclusion of my travel journal was: "The Russians are able to live Communism."[11] But other than including a few Russian authors in our publishing list, further cooperation with the USSR was out of the question at the time.[12]

I found our first European partner, who could be a real candidate for the kind of cooperation I strived for, at the Frankfurt Book Fair in the fall of 1961. Together with Spanish entrepreneurs I founded the book club Círculo de Lectores in Barcelona in 1962. Although my employees and I put a lot of effort into this union, we soon had to face unimaginable difficulties.

Our experiences with a German distribution system did

not entirely transfer to the Spanish market. In many rural areas, we could not simply mail books to the customer. Instead, we had to create a complicated and expensive messenger-delivery system. On top of that, cooperating with our Spanish partners was unexpectedly difficult. At the time the Franco regime was in power, which strictly regulated all social and political life in Spain. The government was distrustful, resentful even, toward foreign publishers. Not surprising, considering that in a country controlled by censorship the import of foreign thought might bring with it the moral and political dissolution of the totalitarian order. Politicians and officials responsible for education, who were faithful to Franco, met us with disdain. *"En España no se lee!"* ("Nobody reads in Spain!") was their battle cry. Admittedly we had underestimated the difficulties in trying to transfer educational materials to an entirely different cultural and political order.

And yet, I was not ready to give up. The first club catalog from October 1962 (with Picasso's *Harlequin* on the title page announcing an art book) offered authors of world literature: Faulkner and Dostoyevsky, Cervantes and Ortega y Gasset, Steinbeck, Hemingway, and many others. The people gobbled it up. The Spanish, who according to their government's assessment didn't like to read at all, flocked to our first foreign club. By 1968, after only six years, Círculo de Lectores had half a million members.

What began as a terra incognita developed into a flourishing cultural landscape. In the following decades the club didn't limit itself to publishing only certain authors, but also organized readings and international author events at *centros culturales* that had been specifically created for this purpose in Madrid and Barcelona. These events were received enthusiastically by the Spanish population.[13]

Following the extraordinarily dynamic growth in Spain, we attempted to move the Círculo de Lectores across the Atlantic. Within ten years, we founded clubs in several Latin American countries.[14] By 1967, the Círculo de Lectores delivered books to about six hundred members in Venezuela; in 1969, we officially founded the Círculo in Mexico; and in 1971, the Círculo de Lectores opened its doors in Argentina. Brazil joined in 1972, and in the following years, the Círculo family included Ecuador, Uruguay, Peru, Chile, and Costa Rica.

The move to Latin America had required a true pioneer spirit. Due to the rudimentary (and sometimes even nonexistent) postal system, we developed a messenger system similar to the one already in place in rural Spain in order to recruit and service members. Some of the most impressive memories of my life are my visits to native villages, where 80 percent of the inhabitants had become avid readers. The educational ministers of these countries were enthusiastic; they had never seen such support for the education of their citizens.

Yet in the end, what was a pioneer achievement in cultural history could not withstand the politically unstable and economically insecure history of South America. Within a few years, the clubs in South America either become integrated parts of new partner businesses or had to be abandoned altogether. Challenges of this magnitude come at a painful price. Our involvement in Latin America has remained, to this day, an important learning experience for us.

Just after we founded the club in Spain's neighbor Portugal in 1974, the so-called carnation revolution broke out. This proved to be a hard test for the Portuguese Círculo. But unlike the clubs in South America, the Portuguese club grew over the decades to be a valuable cultural institution of Portuguese society.

In the mid-1960s, we also established publishing partners in countries neighboring Germany. In 1966, Bertelsmann was involved in the Austrian book club Donauland; in 1970, we founded France Loisirs. In 1968, we began contact with the Italian publisher Tito Legrenzi, who, due to his advanced age, wanted to sell his life's work, the paper factory Cartiere del Garda and the Istituto Italiano d'Arti Grafico. Personally and entrepreneurially, he was a reliable partner for the Bertelsmann expansion in Italy. Even in such different countries as Scandinavia, Israel, and the former Yugoslavia, clubs came into being.

By and large, the growing internationalization of the book clubs brought with it great challenges. Not only did we have to constantly refine the organization of the club structure, we also had to adapt it to the different educational standards and sales landscapes in the various countries. In order to offer enough titles in the host language, we welcomed local publishers in the development of the respective book clubs. This cooperation has been extraordinarily helpful in navigating the national and cultural peculiarities of any host nation. Allow me to note that, from a publisher's point of view, introducing highbrow literature across the globe was possible only due to the high print runs of the book clubs. We were able to help make authors popular in unimaginable ways. Particularly in remote areas in Latin America, where cultural offerings were rare, authors such as Octavio Paz, Ernesto Sabato, and Pablo Neruda have become cult figures, in large part due to the work of the book club.

In the late 1969s and early 1970s, the internationalization of the book clubs presented further challenges to the development of our corporate organization and our ability to manage the Bertelsmann Corporation. In Germany, we continued the process of diversification begun in the 1950s. The purchase of UFA stock from the Deutsche Bank in 1964 established the foundation for our later involvement in film and television (already in its infancy with the creation of the Bertelsmann TV Production Company BFP in 1960). In 1969, we got involved in the newspaper business with a 25 percent acquisition in Gruner+Jahr Verlag in Hamburg. Only four years later, in 1973, our minority involvement became a majority involvement. In the coming decades, Gruner+Jahr would develop into an important part of our corporation.

ENSURING THE QUALITY OF MANAGEMENT

With the fast growth of the Bertelsmann Corporation in diversified industries, management skills and a careful evaluation of their corporate and social consequences became ever-more important. Considering that I had already dealt with leadership issues as a young man, I was quite aware that the style and quality of management had enormous impact on any community. Honestly, it is simply impossible to place too much importance on the ability to lead! In my experience, success, be it of a political, economic, military, or educational institution, is directly related to the quality of leadership. Other factors, such as research, training, product development, administration, sales, organization, and personnel work are a distant second.

Having grown up in the hierarchical structure of National Socialism, and then experiencing the conscious reflections of a young federal democracy, the search for a management technique that would be current with the times occupied me for decades.

Since the beginning of the 1970s, I developed my ideas of the central importance of the quality of leadership and discussed them in numerous notes, essays, and speeches, constantly revising them and elaborating further.[15] It is fundamentally important to distinguish management structure and its methodological practice from personnel questions. Without a doubt, I support a democratic-parliamentarian management style, but this does not mean it is the optimal management technique for any and all situations. There are many well-justified intermediary forms between an authoritarian and a democratic leadership style. Authoritarian management, with which I was personally familiar from Bertelsmann history—its patriarchal yet socially responsible management style—does not offer only disadvantages. A patriarchal structure allows for simple and fast decisions and circumvents any coordination problems, which are a given of the modern decentralized management style. Yet the limits of this leadership style become apparent as soon as the problems become more complex and when corporate decision-making processes need transparency so that corporate continuity is uninterrupted.

Only a democratic decision-making process makes exchange among creative minds possible. And only the exchange of creative minds infuses the management with the necessary input for improvements and innovations that an authoritarian style lacks. It is no coincidence that dictatorial measures garner success in developing countries as long as the challenges consist of relatively simple organizational production problems. It is also no surprise that in these countries socialism goes hand in hand with dictatorship, because a modern leadership style based on the principle of delegating responsibility requires a certain level of education and development that would enable such delegation. If an infrastructure for sharing responsibilities does not exist—as in several African and Asian countries—establishing democratic principles right away is virtually impossible.

In Germany and other industrialized nations of the West, however, an authoritarian leadership style is no longer tenable, and not least due to historical experience. This is as true for the style of leadership in a family as it is for the style of leadership in a larger organization. Our complex, highly developed, and flexible living and working conditions ask too much of an authoritarian leadership style. Furthermore, an authoritarian style no longer corresponds to the self-image of modern man, who seeks individualized fulfillment. Applying such a leadership style today (and this is the case still in quite a few leadership positions) can only be justified by tradition. Ultimately, however, authoritarian management styles are destructive.

The reconstruction years taught me that the delegation of responsibility can release innovation. This is what I wanted to continue, to develop, adjusting it step-by-step to the demands of our growing company. The more I thought about it, the clearer it was to me that management is no longer mere title that comes with the job (as it did in a more traditional understanding of entrepreneurship). Management must be seen as a special skill, which requires development and training, both by way of professional training schools and within corporate human resources departments. I was particularly interested in developing strategies within a company that would foster the development of new leadership techniques. By what standards could we select employees for leadership development? Which qualities, which personality traits, are vital to leadership irrespective of field?

Which traits would be potentially decisive when seeking out, selecting, and developing young managers?

The war and the difficulties of reconstruction afterward had shown me the importance of motivation, and the power of an individual's capacity to commit to a community. I had learned that people can endure and achieve a great deal if they are convinced that they are, in part, acting on their own behalf. To that end it is vital that managers and employees alike, as well as the company's union representatives, understand the behavior and motivation of the corporate leadership. People only really commit to the business endeavors of their company if they believe it is right. Righteousness, however, is never solely defined by power and profit! The humanitarian goals of a company must be clear to the employees as well.

Anyone who wishes to lead in a compassionate fashion has to initiate an ongoing communication with his employees. Anyone who wants to lead has the obligation to keep his employees informed and to offer assistance whenever necessary. Anyone who wants to lead has to set an example and strive for a fair balance of interests. What was most important to me in these matters was a close cooperation with our company's union representatives based on mutual trust and respect. Therefore, I always insisted on personally discussing important issues with the union representatives, and on personally presenting these issues at union meetings. To this day I am close to one of the company union directors: Jochen Werner! His open and honest yet critical attitude spiced up many a discussion and had quite an impact on consensus building at the Bertelsmann Corporation. He was a well-liked advisor to the Bertelsmann board of directors.

The willingness to maintain a dialogue avoids the ultimately costly and destructive "culture of combat." I wanted to keep the culture of partnership based on mutual respect that we had built in the two postwar decades, even now in the era of globalization. When older employees tell me today that during those tempestuous postwar years they would have gone through fire for me, I can answer with joy and gratitude that I would have done the same for them, and probably have more often than once.[16] We were partners, and it is this spirit upon which we built the entire company. I have always been convinced that an economically successful entrepreneur—no matter how large or small his company—has to be ready to take social responsibility for the people under his charge. Therefore, Bertelsmann established a solid health plan, which gave security to our employees. But I wanted more. I kept coming back to the concept of profit sharing we had initiated in the 1950s, and I was looking for ways to reconcile the demands on our employees' performance with the economic success of our company. This turned out to be an ongoing process, and therefore, management, employees, and I constantly questioned, developed, and revised the corporate culture of the Bertelsmann Corporation that had first been defined in 1960. Our various foreign experiences with a wide range of political systems had confirmed my initial assumption that the delegation of responsibility, personal motivation, and individual commitment to corporate goals are more successful than a fixation on power and profit. The basic tenets of our corporate culture—fulfilling a duty toward humanity, respectful reconciliation of employee and corporate interests, and adhering to the principle of justice—turned out to be an advantage in the foreign markets.

Bertelsmann's extraordinary success in the 1960s and 1970s, not only in Germany but throughout the world, would not have been possible without the model of cooperation based on mutual trust between management and employees. After all, most of the employees hailed from the participating countries. If we wanted to grow further, we had to delegate responsibilities further as well—to the lower levels of management. This in turn meant constant training of management personnel. The more I thought about it, the more it became evident that one vital criterion for the selection of employees with leadership qualities had to be the employee's willingness to accept and commit to our corporate constitution and goals.

Now I know that the capacity to lead well is the most important factor of a company's success. And I have learned that, if you are striving for continued success, even the best leadership needs constant training. The larger a company, the higher the level of refinement on the managerial, legal, and organizational levels. It is the human factor that tips the scale!

A QUESTION OF PERSONALITY

Naturally, in the course of my life I've met many interesting people, among them politicians and entrepreneurs with great ideas. Yet time separates the wheat from the chaff. When all is said and done, only those with extraordinary integrity and unwavering human nobility have taken an eternal place in my memory. People like that are rare, and I feel fortunate to have met them.

One of them I met in France. My attempts to cooperate with the publisher Hachette had been unsuccessful. Careful market research in 1967 had shown the promising possibilities of the French market, but Hachette decided to go at it alone, without a German partner.[17] Hachette bought a smaller book club, but in the end they didn't succeed due to an insufficient organizational structure. My hope of establishing a book club in France had been delayed but was by no means discarded. I finally contacted Presses de la Cité and asked for a meeting with their publisher, Sven Nielsen. At the time Bertelsmann's work with book clubs was already well known throughout Europe, and so Sven Nielsen agreed to meet me right away. And a few days later we sat face-to-face in his Paris offices to discuss my ideas.

The meeting was very congenial. Originally from Denmark, Sven Nielsen was married to a woman who had fought in the Résistance and who was friends with the Mitterand family. His bearing showed him to be a gentleman of old Europe. I outlined my thoughts on a two-step book club, and persuaded him so completely that we agreed to cooperate then and there. The only remaining question was which end of the partnership would lead the operation. I argued that my years of experience with, and knowledge of, the book club business was a good reason to make Bertelsmann the managing partner. Mr. Nielsen, however, argued that in a good partnership, an equal distribution of responsibilities would be more appropriate.

This was a difficult decision for me. I was not easily persuaded. I asked for a day to think it over. I thought long and hard that evening. No doubt, Nielsen had made a strong impression on me. The next morning I decided to trust him and agreed.

Together we drew up an agreement that outlined the decision-making process step by step. But never once did we have to refer to this agreement. The years of cooperation that followed are some of my most cherished professional memories. Our meetings were always very congenial, we were in tune with each other, and our relationship was crowned with success.[18] The Club France Loisirs, founded in 1970, performed exceptionally well. Several years later, just before Christmas, I received an invitation to join Sven Nielsen at his hunting castle just south of Paris. This meant interrupting my own winter vacation, but I didn't let my annoyance get in the way and ended up enjoying a generous and joyful evening among friends. In the end each of us took home the pheasant he had shot that day. We were in good spirits!

A few days later, while I was back on my winter vacation, I received a call from my manager in France: Sven Nielsen had suddenly passed away due to a severe illness. His contract with France Loisirs expired at the end of that year. Upstanding as he was, he had wanted to fulfill his professional obligations to me, and then he bid me adieu with the invitation to his hunting castle.

This touched me deeply. I would have liked to work with a man like Sven Nielsen my entire life. He had been a reliable friend all those years. His personality had shown me that contracts and agreements have their place in professional life, but they cannot replace personal integrity, mutual trust, and respect.

In over two decades after World War II, during the years of reconstruction and the years of the growing internationalization of Bertelsmann, I met a wide variety of people all over the globe and engaged in dialogue with them. My generation had to deal with an unavoidable historic situation, in that victims of the Holocaust had to live and work together with former members of the German army. This released difficult emotions for everyone involved, as both sides attempted to bridge the abyss of the past to build a future together. Conversations were not always possible. Building bridges to the present was not always possible. But when it was, it was an unforgettable experience, which has given me strength for all that the future might hold.

In the latter half of the 1970s, I took up an offer to buy the Italian publisher Fabbri. As we prepared the contracts, the seller also offered the American pocket book chain Bantam Books to me. This was an offer to buy the largest pocket book publisher in the United States, and it was an opportunity I didn't want to miss. We signed the contract, and shortly thereafter I flew to New York to meet with the publisher, Oscar Dystel, and with his managers at Bantam Books.

The time for this first meeting was set for 8 a.m. Being an early riser, this was not a problem for me. But it was certainly unusual. The early meeting time turned out to be an omen for a rather harsh welcome. As Oscar Dystel and his managers entered the meeting room, the atmosphere turned icy. Without any decorum, the publisher asked me bluntly what I was doing here. As it turned out, his question had nothing to do with a perceived obscurity of the sales agreement. The question referred to my nationality. Oscar Dystel was Jewish, and in me he saw a representative of a murderous regime, one with the audacity to act like the owner of an American publisher. We looked at each other. It was clear to me that very instant that I'd have to ignore my calendar for the next few days. "I want to talk to you," I said. And we did.

Over the next five days and nights, Oscar Dystel, his managers, and I discussed matters. I told them about my youth in National Socialist Germany, about my war experiences, about my time at the Concordia prison camp and all it had meant to me. And I told him why I believed that the development of a corporate culture must go hand-in-hand with the development of democracy in Germany. In the end he said, "Have you ever been to the book fair in Jerusalem? You have to go there." We became friends. With Oscar Dystel's help, I learned about the difficult conditions in Israel, and I met the mayor of Jerusalem, Teddy Kollek—a fantastic person. It was this meeting that kicked off the decade-long engagement of the Bertelsmann Foundation in Israel. But this is a story for a different context.

MOTIVATION AND COMMITMENT
IN A LARGE CORPORATION

Ever since the first postwar decade, our company expanded steadily. By the 1960s, Bertelsmann had become more and more international as well. Then, in 1971, we turned what had been a midsize company into a management-driven media corporation with the foundation of the Bertelsmann AG. Now it was my responsibility to make sure that the building blocks of our company culture would carry over to the structure of a large corporation. And indeed, what I had originally developed for a midsize company would prove perfectly tenable for the international Bertelsmann Corporation as well.[19]

I still wanted to combine the leadership qualities we had developed so successfully in the postwar years—personal motivation, creativity and courage, human respect and good judgment—with the entrepreneurial freedom that had naturally flowed from the delegation of responsibility. I wanted to pass on what I had personally experienced: "learning by doing," in other words, allowing for mistakes as long as they are reflected upon and can therefore be avoided in the future. At the same time, I assumed that my irrevocable demand that management accept the goals and values of the corporation, placing them above all other efforts, would be a far greater challenge in a large corporation than in a midsize company. After all, the goals of a midsize company are far more comprehensible and transparent where the personal contact between management and employees is still possible.

Based on my experiences in the first years after the war, and driven by the ethics of my entrepreneurial self-image, I concluded that profit maximization and capital gain would not suffice as an entrepreneurial objective of the Bertelsmann Corporation. Even under the conditions of a large corporation, I wanted to maintain the tenets of the corporate culture we had outlined in the 1950s and first stipulated in the 1960s. The human being was still to be the center of any future development of the Bertelsmann Corporation.

There is no doubt that the ever-growing size of the company placed ever-growing demands on its leadership. The company regulations regarding tax, antitrust, and social laws from the 1960s and the 1970s, as well as the growing need for capital that would ensure the company's competitive edge, could no longer be satisfied by sole ownership. We had to find alternative corporate finance. The broad distribution of capital harbored the risk that stockholder interest would no longer be that of the corporate leadership. Leading the corporation successfully under these newly challenging circumstances placed high demands on the recruitment of qualified management personnel. Ownership of capital could no longer justify leadership. In the future, a legitimate claim to lead would have to be justified solely by a display of leadership qualities that would guarantee the successful handling of the entrepreneurial responsibilities.

My experiences during the period of our corporate development had taught me that an optimal organization of the work process depends greatly on the creative potential of the individual. Of course, my courage to grant liberties and delegate responsibility to employees was put to the test once in a while. Yet in my experience, there was no alternative. To this day I firmly believe that the delegation of responsibility is the key to entrepreneurial innovation.

Within this larger corporation I wanted to foster the positive company atmosphere that had developed from the respectful interaction within Bertelsmann in the 1950s. Yet fostering the independence of employees requires not only that the corporate goals be continuously communicated, but also that the processes of such company-wide communication be questioned and constantly improved. In the 1970s, we researched several tools that would accomplish these goals, and in 1977, we introduced regular employee surveys. These surveys can only be implemented by way of respectful cooperation between the corporate leadership and the company union representatives. That way employees can express their experiences and pass on information to the corporate leaders without fear of reprisals from their immediate superiors. Repeating these surveys regularly ensures that problems are actually addressed. This transparent monitoring system in turn supports the willingness to communicate and cooperate within a corporation. To this day employee surveys are among the most effective leadership tools within the Bertelsmann Corporation.

In my opinion, the independence of our employees plays an extraordinarily important role with regard to the optimization of the working process. This encouraged me to explore whether a certain income distribution would also foster independence. I wanted to find out whether the high work ethic characterizing the self-employed could somehow be translated to the employees of a large corporation. And so I went back to the principle of profit sharing, which we had tested in the 1950s, albeit now on a much larger scale (exceeding the national and company-wide wage scale). I decided to guarantee profit sharing for every employee at Bertelsmann. I was certain that the future challenges of such a dynamic corporation could only be met if its employees could support its goals, and do so without hesitation. And I was convinced that, if such support is to be more than just lip service, fiscal fairness would be a prerequisite.

THE NEED FOR COMPETITION IN A DEMOCRACY AND A MARKET ECONOMY

Although the demands of my average work day in the 1970s left little time for leisure, I had not abandoned my old habit of carefully reflecting upon entrepreneurial decisions by myself. I wanted to use my rich experiences in those first two postwar decades as a source for the further reorganization of Bertelsmann. On my many walks I would reflect upon the social, political, and economic development of the Federal Republic of Germany. Bertelsmann had undergone an impressive entrepreneurial overhaul after the destruction of the war. The successes of the book clubs and their later expansion were proof that, if their needs were recognized and addressed by a company, people were willing to forge new paths even in hard times. People want progress![20]

In the wake of the internationalization of our company, I encountered rather different political systems and national interests in my entrepreneurial work. Obviously this had great impact on our entrepreneurial initiatives. This was food for thought with regard to the development in our own country. It seemed to me Germany's seemingly outdated constitutional regulations remained in place even during the years of reconstruction.

The influence of the Allied occupying forces was not always helpful. It was Ludwig Erhard's reforms that established the regulations of the socially responsible free-market

economy, which turned out to be a blessing for the development of democratic Germany. Instead of protectionism
that would shield the national market (a principle that had
been in place all over Europe before the war), the new principle was an encompassing trade liberalization. And it bore
fruit quickly. In the postwar decades, Western Europe was
characterized by an extraordinary increase of productivity,
along with the migration that naturally follows.[21]

By comparison, the conditions of production in communist Eastern Europe fell far behind. The abyss between
East and West widened ever more due to a lopsided focus
on heavy industries and on monopolized structures rig-
idly managed by the state. The planned economy on the
other side of the Iron Curtain was heavy-handed. The
state determined and controlled the means of production
and their distribution among the population. Often it took
years for public criticism of the state of affairs to result in
changes.

Western European nations, on the other hand, had created
many expectations that had to be fulfilled.[22] The network of
social privileges and economic strategies developed in the
wake of economic growth had led to the common belief
that the state served its citizens, rather than vice versa. The
welfare state of the Federal Republic of Germany, which expanded continuously throughout the 1960s and 1970s, was a
well-cushioned system for both citizens and public officials.
But then the social privileges that characterized the welfare

state were gradually seen as indispensable necessities that deserved protection at any cost. It seemed as if Germany was well on its way to becoming a "parasitic society."[23]

In critical contemplation of the German postwar situation, I have to admit that the healthy competition, which encouraged me and other entrepreneurs to pursue ever-new and better performance standards, was nonexistent in state administration and politics. Too late did the Federal Republic of Germany establish dearly needed policies of reform. After World War II, material needs were of utmost importance, so that the political, social, and economic focus did not necessarily strive for the strongest organizational system.[24] The path toward a European Union was paved with many different national ideas. In the 1970s, the European idea was far from being realized.

The responsible politicians did not question themselves with the same rigor that I used when questioning my own decisions and goals. Why? Which historical and cultural reasons could lead to stagnation only two decades after the establishment of a new Federal Republic of Germany? Why was it that, while the concepts of democracy and market economy were based on a responsible citizenry, the state did not really leave room for that same citizenry to take responsibility and exert influence?[25]

Granted, I had seen conditions that were worse than those that had developed in Germany. But I had also seen encouraging examples: institutions that seemed more efficient and humane than those in Germany.

Careful historical research made it clear to me that, despite war and destruction, the German administration even after 1945 was still anchored in the Prussian traditions, which reach back as far as the eighteenth and nineteenth centuries. With virtually no adjustments, the state's objective was still to protect the order it had created. While the German economy had been impacted by the powerful spirit of change and competition in the first two postwar decades, the German administration had remained virtually untouched by it.

The success of a company like Bertelsmann during the difficult years of reconstruction and early internationalization proves that people all over the world strive for better living conditions and personal progress, as long as the means used to reach those goals are persuasive. Entrepreneurial competition is what drove this engine, and in the end it was the people themselves who were the decisive factor as to which of the competing models should win.

The desire for freedom and self-determination demanded that economic leaders become personally engaged in the pursuit of common goals and common affiliation with these goals. Why was this not working in the public sphere? Without a doubt, the monopolistic structure of the administration had created a sense of entitlement with disastrous consequences.

Throughout the 1970s and thereafter, the majority of higher-level state officials were mainly interested in keeping the rights and privileges to which they, as government employees, were entitled (especially considering that these rights and privileges allowed for rather comfortable living and working conditions). The income of leading public service officials was not based on performance or competition. It was therefore not a surprise that public servants were more interested in maintaining the status quo than in meeting the interests of the citizens and their changing needs. It is impossible to maintain competent leadership that way! This attitude left no room for change and competition. The citizens relied on the state; but policies were based on subjectivity and personal interests, and there was no monitoring system in place that would check their efficiency and usefulness. Without competition, there was no transparency and no regulation that would give a modicum of control to the citizens. It remains doubtful that the huge financial needs of the state were spent in the interests of the citizens, or in the best possible way.

The unions should take some of the blame, too. For years they manipulated public opinion, which could have positively affected partial codetermination and thus changed the structure of state and economy. In my opinion, the unions were guided by a desire to maintain power. This should never be tolerated by critical citizens. The desired parity would, in the long run, lead to poor entrepreneurial leadership, decrease of productivity, and a lower standard of living. The development of the unions in Yugoslavia in the 1970s exemplifies that.

For decades I have discussed my social politics with

representatives of the union, openly and critically debating all issues regarding wage scales, codetermination, and corporate capital gain. Despite many disagreements, leading union representatives recognized that the social models of the Bertelsmann Corporation offered a quality of "pioneering solutions" that could jump-start general path-breaking initiatives for social change.[26]

Without a doubt, Germany had developed into a stable democracy in the two or more decades after World War II. And as is true in all cultures of this world, the administrators showed a tendency to protect their achievements and accomplishments. My experiences had taught me, however, that only the power of competition can guarantee the quality of the leaders and their achievements. But in the political debates of the time, this argument was not viewed favorably. The idea that all it took was a multiparty system to guarantee a fair balance of interests was rather popular. I was convinced, on the other hand, that democracy as a system based on the will of the people needs constant revisions if it wants to outperform autocratic and totalitarian systems. The quality of our political leadership had to be addressed and discussed publicly. For a common characteristic of monopolistic state-run companies is weak leadership and low productivity. Therefore it was vital to overcome the lack of efficiency and to reform the top-heavy bureaucracies.

In my youth I had experienced that the desire for power of a criminal clique can lead to disaster. In order to secure a free democracy, and to guarantee its acceptance and stability by its citizens, the institutions must be monitored continuously. Without a monitoring system, political petrification and public disappointment follow—with dangerous political consequences.

Although I didn't quite foresee the social, political, and economic consequences of such stagnation, I felt uncomfortable with the political development in Germany. As a young entrepreneur, I often noticed that the quality of many economic processes could have been improved in a way the government didn't necessarily support. But far worse, many seeds sown by the dynamic economic development in Germany fell on barren administrative soil.

PROGRESS NEEDS FREEDOM

The more I reflected upon the premise of economic and political action, the more I was preoccupied with human nature. Who are we? Which constants determine our being, and which freedoms, if any, can we create for ourselves through education and action?

Even today Europe holds the notion that the basic tenets of our Western civilization are rooted in the Renaissance. The Renaissance was a time of a cultural high, characterized by a return to the values of antiquity paired with the dawn of individualism. The philosophical ideas of the era opened the door to the age of enlightenment, which in turn was characterized by the separation of church and state, the proclamation of Human Rights, and the idea of freedom.

All this is true and right, and yet the history of Western values has also been influenced by insights from times much further removed, insights originating in the culture of the Mediterranean between the ninth and fifteenth centuries. And it is no coincidence that it was mainly traders and entrepreneurs who brought Islamic and Christian achievements together in the flourishing Italian city-states, mainly in Venice, the most important cosmopolitan center at the time.[27] It was under Islamic and Christian rule that the free arts and sciences developed: philosophy and medicine, logic and mathematics, poetry and cartography.

The many different cultural influences generated a lively mix of sometimes opposing convictions. Debates about God, rationalism, morality, and individuality, influenced by Islamic thinkers such as Ibn Sina and Ibn Rushd and Western thinkers such as Aristotle and Plato, fostered the liberation from the dogma of the Middle Ages and encouraged the shift toward the European Renaissance. What seems like a single stream today was really a rather lively river fed by many tributaries coming from a long-forgotten source.[28]

Throughout history, cultures have developed through the prism of human experiences. Throughout history, communities have been maintained and defended on the basis of the values generated in these cultures. The cultures had to undergo revisions as they faced many influences and learning processes, which in critical phases could even lead to radical cultural changes. Over thousands of years, military power and territorialism have defined cultures. But it is impossible to maintain power forever by force alone. Eventually people will rise up and topple the rule of incompetent leaders, risking life and limb, all in an effort to improve their living conditions.

Hegel's notion of the "spirit" led to the notion of a national culture in the nineteenth century, a notion that would influence political discourse far into the twentieth century.[29] Two world wars and unfathomable human suffering were among the disastrous consequences of this national idea, which aims to stabilize itself through internal coherence and external differentiation. The national state defines itself as much by its own national heroes as it does by its enemies, thus ignoring any and all differentiating correlations. The national state lays claim to art, science, and research, negating everything that would challenge its exclusive claim.

The beautiful yet idealistic notion of a homogenous national culture shows its dark side when it has to exclude and reject any and all foreign influences. Only the stability of our culture seems to secure our identity, and yet it is stability that reveals itself as its greatest enemy! For it is precisely the desire for a homogenous culture that opens the door to violence and retribution. People fight one another, accepting that they have to destroy what is foreign in order to secure their own national interests. Those who reject what is foreign ultimately deny the very origin of all cultures—the meeting and melting of different sources and influences—and close their eyes to historical truth, which no nation and no continent can call its own.

Unlike national thinkers and rulers, traders and businessmen have always crossed national borders and traveled in foreign cultures in order to bring home new goods and discoveries. In fact, trade was driven by the inspiration of foreign cultures: Traders became aware of foreign products that would eventually aid the development of their own culture, which, in turn, would promise both the trader and his customer welfare and progress. It was Voltaire who had proclaimed our duty to understand all those with whom we share a planet, tying his ethical command directly to our mutual economic dependency.[30]

History shows that flourishing cultural centers developed where trade routes converged. The rise of the city of Alexandria and the thriving metropolis of Venice exemplify the vitality and dynamic power of competition, which thrives from the interplay of cultures rather than their mutual exclusion. Time and again history illustrates that the downfall of a culture is equated with the abuse of power by a ruling class, which no longer acknowledges the needs of its citizens, or deliberately disregards them, thereby hindering their own culture's development. This generally results in either external or internal upheavals that eventually force the culture to either embrace progress or face its own doom.

The history of mankind shows that no static culture has ever persisted. This would not be desirable anyway. A culture that continuously revises and renews its tenets in general and its intellectual orientation in particular is more successful than a culture that upholds its dogmas. The

premises of a culture must align with human progress, for
the desire for progress and better living standards is part
of human nature, and the desire for a positive self-image
is one of the invariable motivators for human action. Our
need to adjust to the circumstances of our lives and to gain
the respect of others is inextricably bound to the large array
of values we've acquired, consciously or unconsciously, to
guide our daily behavior.

The need for values is innate in all people of all cultures.
It is only the content of such values that varies based on
cultural and historical circumstances. This originates in our
need to perceive moral significance in our deeds—the same
impulse that guides us in our search for spiritual and religious meaning. And so it is no coincidence that all cultures
in the world have been influenced by religion. Religions
strive to offer people spiritual orientation, personal help,
and a sense of community. Without this sense of community, peace is not possible. Peace is the most important ethical and religious task of the great churches of the world. The
cultural variables of any spiritual orientation need to show
willingness for intercultural dialogue. Every human society
must anchor its belief system in justice, defining its order
in a basic law. This legal basis, of course, must undergo
the same changes as the values themselves. Only a cultural
openness can release the self-renewing power that can influence any and all human systems of order. Anyone who
takes this openness seriously will recognize that granting
freedom of thought is the best possible protection against

willfulness and other dangers. Only freedom and creativity can protect progress and survival! This insight harbors the courage for change, providing man with a chance for self-determination.

Within the past two thousand years we can find numerous instances of the exemplary power of free enterprise. Where cultural openness was combined with a performance-directed ethic, success would follow. That such dynamic growth in Europe could spring from the ruins of two world wars is unthinkable without the impulses of a strong economy and resourceful entrepreneurs. While in the 1950s politicians still placed their faith in national ideas, economic leaders had long started to make contacts in foreign countries and to pursue forms of cooperation that in Germany would not have been possible due to antitrust laws.

After World War II, the power of the exchange initiated by the economy bloomed socially and politically. The success of Bertelsmann's involvement in Spain and Latin America, for example, allowed us glimpses of societies that at the time were not possible by political means. I often remembered my experiences with American citizens, collected during my years as a POW, and subsequently confirmed later on many entrepreneurial trips. Compared to America, the potential of the mature citizen remained untapped in Germany. The dire need for political and social reform was obvious. I was inspired by my experiences with Bertelsmann's foreign involvement. I wanted to use these positive examples to the advantage of the German people. So

I began to search for effective tools to foster an international comparison of social and political institutions.

THE SIGNIFICANCE OF SPIRITUAL ORIENTATION FOR STATE AND SOCIETY

In the 1970s, recollections of the various stages of our entrepreneurial development convinced me that our model of corporate culture, which was based on creativity, personal motivation, and commitment, could contribute to the democratic culture of our country. Much of Bertelsmann's success harks back to the following four clear leadership principles:

1. Social justification of entrepreneurial goals

2. Deeply rooted employee commitment to entrepreneurial action

3. Far-reaching delegation of responsibility

4. A leadership style based on partnership and performance

I intended to apply these important entrepreneurial strengths to society as well. Transferred to the democratic development of the Federal Republic of Germany, application of these leadership principles meant that the citizens of our country would identify with the goals and actions of the state, thereby exerting influence responsibly; that in an equal partnership between state and citizen, citizens could expect state performance geared toward the benefit of the citizenry—they themselves performing for the benefit of the common good. Was this realistic? Was it not precisely in these areas where much work was to be done?

The more I thought about this, the more I was convinced that the performance of our state would define the political stability as well as the quality of life of the next generation. The history of mankind, and not least the catastrophic developments in the first half of the twentieth century, had clearly shown that political systems not guided by ethical rules and basic legal tenets end in violence and anarchy. As opposed to the hierarchical order of violent totalitarianism witnessed in the first half of the twentieth century, society after 1945 developed toward a growing liberalization with far-reaching consequences for democracy. The tenets of personal freedom and individual self-determination so popular in the 1960s and 1970s challenged the very basis of German society and redefined its notion of humanity/compassion.

The role of the citizen was changing, and this change posed many questions.[31] What would be the foundations of our future society? How could the view back through the history of the West be helpful? Did individual religious education play a role in the stability of a democratic order? The former definition of the state, intended to maintain order, was rooted in hierarchical worldviews that saw the citizen as subject to the power of the state. The objectives of the modern state had to be redefined and, in its service function, find guidance in the standard of international competition. By the same token, however, the duties of the citizen in such a democratic state are to take social responsibility and to personally work toward the common good. The social changes brought about in the late 1960s reverberate even to this day.

An enormously improved quality of life had, in many sectors of society, led to the notion that learning ethical behavior was insignificant. The rebellion against hierarchical structures, however justified, during the revolts in 1968 developed into aimless liberalization that questioned any commonly held value system of a democratic society.

As a youth I had suffered from the strict religious discipline in my parents' home, thereby missing the personal motivation that comes with inner conviction, as well as the critical dialogue that openly debates all questions while respecting both points of view. Yet the challenges I had to face as a young man widened my horizons. As a young officer and as a young entrepreneur, I had to lead people in difficult situations and learned that no matter what age, people search for spiritual guidance because they want to find common ground with the goals of their community. And my experiences abroad convinced me that our democracy, built on catastrophic historical premises, would not last without professing a spiritual orientation.

At the time it became clear to me that it is one's spiritual orientation that informs the connection between individual and society, defining the level of commitment on moral grounds. Spiritual guidance places an individual within his society and encourages him to take social responsibility. It is human nature to safeguard one's life and protect one's community. History has taught us that people are quite willing to change their habits if that change is necessary to attain such goals. But such change costs time and money, and can only be realized if those affected clearly see the need for it.

Scientific progress and insight into the conditions of economic competition can make these needs apparent. The political leadership has the duty to persuade its citizens. This is a difficult task, particularly in a democratic society! If the leadership cannot effect such change due to hierarchical or dogmatic premises, the very existence of the culture is at stake. For the strength to maintain a culture from "above" is limited; culture is, or should be, a democratic process. But only if we are convinced that our personal welfare is identical to the welfare of our community will we be motivated and committed to the very welfare of that society. Only then can we willingly provide new impulses and ideas, thereby releasing the necessary power for a renewal of our spiritual orientation.

When discussing the development of values and goals and the assertion of humanity, it is vital to consider the significance of religion as spiritual guideline. Not only the state but the churches as well must rethink their roles for the future. In the last few decades the cooperation of church and politics has come to a standstill. Yet it is only through cooperation of church and state that a reform of ethics, spiritual welfare, and humanity is possible. Ethics and faith are facing a particular challenge now and must seek out a critical dialogue with people. It is impossible to persuade people in questions of faith without mutual understanding and trust. The representatives of religion have to regain their followers' trust and realign their faith with their behavior. The connection between doctrine, commitment, and faith cannot be underestimated. People have to understand the basics of their spiritual orientation. Dogmas without justification have no room in modern society. A comparative look at different cultures illustrates that people need spiritual orientation to maintain the necessary motivation to live their lives in freedom, while also doing their part in the creation and protection of a free society. To create and protect their society, people first have to understand the goals of their society and be allowed to question them critically.

These were the thoughts that, in 1977, persuaded me to initiate a foundation, which would show political and social leaders that measurable performance standards are significant and useful. Based on my entrepreneurial experiences, I was certain that reforms in large institutions, be they economic, political, military, or religious, would take decades. But I was hopeful that with the help of the Bertelsmann Foundation we would be able to foster social reform processes in the areas of health, education, and administration.[32]

THE POLITICAL FOUNDATIONS OF THE FUTURE: HUMANITY AND JUSTICE

The idea of humanity aims at the equality of all humans regardless of origin or gender. It incorporates human dignity and a notion of pacifism that rejects military preemption, striving for religious and political tolerance. Humanity is the basis for Human Rights and for the Law of Nations; therefore, humanity is the basis of both national and international law. Humanity is anchored deeply in the constitutions of democratic states. It constitutes the basis of any democratic society, founded upon the inalienable rights of respect for one another's interests and the freedom of speech.

Where people meet, work, and live together, the notion of common values comes into play. Anyone who, like me, has seen a great variety of habits and customs while traveling, understands the enormous potential of confronting what is foreign to us, of exchanging experiences with another culture.

Exchanging experiences with foreign cultures teaches us that there are both universal values and values rooted in local custom. Only thorough and open conversations can distinguish one from the other. Meeting people from other cultures widens our horizon, and we catch a glimpse of the great variety of human lifestyles. But we also see what connects them all: the roots of humanity innate in virtually all cultures.[33]

In a democratic culture, which strives to utilize and fulfill the potential of its citizens, the goals set by the political leadership have to generate acceptance while also allowing a certain amount of freedom for personal initiatives. It is the politician's duty to initiate and guide new opportunities. History has taught us that the state's influence can be either positive or negative. Too much influence from the state hinders the cultural development of its citizens. Too little influence from the state hinders the communal orientation of a society.

Based on the experiences of our entrepreneurial beginnings, I saw the social and political management of a community as a manifold process. By engaging in a critical dialogue with citizens, competent personalities, scientists, and state and private institutions, political leaders could initiate ongoing change and further development, benefiting the entire process. The foundation of the Bertelsmann Corporation had followed carefully considered economic and social ideas. Likewise, the setup of the Bertelsmann Foundation was based on two basic goals.

The first goal was to secure the continuity of the corporation. The contracts signed in 1977 stipulated that at a later time the foundation would take over the capital of the Mohn family, and thus would guarantee the financial continuity of the Bertelsmann Corporation free of inheritance tax.

The second goal had more to do with the democratic commitment of all citizens that I had demanded so often. The Bertelsmann Foundation wanted to foster the personal responsibility of every individual, to encourage them all, each to his or her own ability, to participate in the definition and development of the democratic state. The Bertelsmann Foundation was conceived as an institution involved with many international projects, operating predominantly on a conceptual level. The foundation would cooperate with scientists and specialists in different subject areas, while maintaining close contact with both private and government institutions. In the more than thirty years since the foundation's inception, hundreds of projects grew that created exemplary models, inspiring social impulses in such varied fields as economics, politics, administration, education, school and library media, culture, and medicine. As a result of the foundation's work, there have been significant changes in individual participation in the public sphere. The Bertelsmann Foundation was able to demonstrate the need for the reform of state-run institutions and to initiate pioneering changes by contrasting the development and performance of similar institutions in other countries. It remains an objective of the Bertelsmann Foundation to compare and contrast the performance of all countries and to foster progress by initiating a dialogue among democracies.

To me personally, the initiatives of the Bertelsmann Foundation demonstrate the practical democratic involvement I had dreamt of since my time at the Concordia POW camp. Striving for a direct, populist involvement in social developments of the modern state, the projects of the foundation could examine ways that would make democracy more efficient and capitalism more human. In the wake of globalization, what started in the 1970s has reached far beyond German borders. The demand to take a political stand and act politically reaches all of us. We all have to work toward just participation and integration in an ever more global world. Initiated by the projects of the foundation, the critical dialogue with competent cultural, scientific, economic, and political leaders has always been a source of reflection to me. Even today the foundation's strategy focuses on the basic issues of humanity and justice within political and social systems of the world.

Reinhard Mohn, 1929. *(Unternehmensarchiv Bertelsmann AG)*

Heinrich Mohn, c. 1945.
*(Unternehmensarchiv
Bertelsmann AG)*

Agnes Mohn, 1920.
*(Unternehmensarchiv
Bertelsmann AG)*

Reinhard Mohn, guarding a mountain pass in the late 1930s. *(Unternehmensarchiv Bertelsmann AG)*

Reinhard Mohn, c. 1940. *(Unternehmensarchiv Bertelsmann AG)*

Reinhard Mohn, speaking to a crowd in his military coat, January 2, 1947.
(Unternehmensarchiv Bertelsmann AG)

Reinhard Mohn, New York, August 1954.
(Unternehmensarchiv Bertelsmann AG)

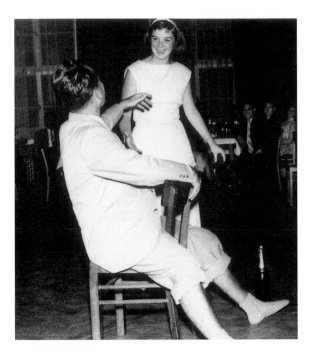

First meeting
between Liz and
Reinhard Mohn, at a
company party, 1957.
*(Unternehmensarchiv
Bertelsmann AG)*

A business lunch on a trip to Japan, May 1963.
(Unternehmensarchiv Bertelsmann AG)

Reinhard Mohn with Oscar Dystel in New York, 1970. *(Bertelsmann AG)*

Reinhard Mohn on
the Vespa of Círculo
de Lectores, 1967.
(Bertelsmann AG)

German President Roman Herzog presenting the Bundesverdienstkreuz (Federal Merit Cross) to Reinhard Mohn, September 10, 1998. (*Bertelsmann Stiftung*)

Liz Mohn, Reinhard Mohn, and Jerusalem Mayor Teddy Kollek at Reinhard Mohn's seventieth birthday celebration, Gütersloh City Hall, July 1, 1991. (*Bertelsmann Stiftung*)

Liz and Reinhard Mohn in the foyer of the Bertelsmann Foundation, Gütersloh, October 7, 2000. *(Bertelsmann Stiftung, Foto-Zeidler, Rheda-Wiedenbrück)*

ON THE ROAD
INTO THE FUTURE

MAKING PERSONAL DECISIONS AND
SETTING AN ENTREPRENEURIAL COURSE

The inception and development of the Bertelsmann Foundation have always been inextricably bound with the concept of partnership, which since the 1950s we had developed from the building blocks of our corporate culture. When in 1974 we laid the foundation for the new headquarters in Gütersloh, we put a roof over our entrepreneurial objectives that combined tradition with worldwide goals. Moving into these new buildings in 1976, we confirmed Gütersloh as the location for our new headquarters, which sent a signal in that direction.

In the Bertelsmann GmbH, we combined eleven separate publishing houses under one roof. Additionally, we founded an encyclopedia publishing house, acquired several other reference publishers, embraced international participation in print and publishing (most important, the publisher Plaza y Janés in Barcelona and Bantam Books in New York), and initiated forays into the international music market and media business by founding Ariola America and acquiring Arista Records in the United States and Great Britain. All this was under my leadership in the 1970s. The course for an international orientation of the corporation had been set when, in 1981, at the age of sixty, I stepped down as CEO and became chairman of the Supervisory Board of the Bertelsmann AG.

With this professional shift, I also began a phase of contemplation and renewal in my personal life. Granted, as a chairman of the Supervisory Board, I continued to follow the expansion of the corporation in the United States and the growing expansion of the radio and TV business (which would eventually develop into an important part of the corporation). But unlike the fast pace of my entrepreneurial days as CEO, the more moderate pace allowed me to reflect upon the development of the Bertelsmann Corporation and its corporate culture as a whole. I had defined this corporate culture in many speeches and company and corporate constitutions and wanted to revise and expand with a view toward social developments and issues. This resulted in several publications.[1]

The Bertelsmann constitution as defined in 1960 already argued for the delegation of responsibility as one of the most important building blocks of our corporate culture. I have never regretted this decision. The development of a large corporation is a long process, over many years, which, if it is to be successful, requires creative exchange and unwavering motivation and commitment. Personal disagreements, mistakes, and disappointments are unavoidable when people work together, searching for the best and most tenable solutions. I am and always have been of the firm conviction that it is vital to first meet your employees and managers with respect and trust in order to release the power of motivation and commitment to the objectives of the corporation. If there are differences, and if these differences cannot be reconciled in conversations, the consequences are clear. That, too, is part of an entrepreneur's responsibility toward the objectives of the company. This has been exemplified as part of the corporate culture defined by the Bertelsmann Corporation in past decades and continually developed in creative exchanges with our employees.

There are moments in the life of every individual when we reflect upon and reevaluate the decisions we have made and the course we have set. More often than not, these are moments when we are acutely aware of our own mortality, and where pure reflection no longer helps. Moments we can only handle with the help of God and a merciful fate. As a young soldier, I had had to live through many situations of life and death. Since that time, great fear has been foreign to me. On my many travels to foreign countries I faced many a difficult situation, but most of them could be handled easily and soon afterward were forgotten.

Once, during a winter flight on the company jet from Stuttgart to Milan, the pilot lost control of the plane somewhere in the Alps. Although we had taken off in a snowstorm and vision was limited, the pilot was confident that the flight would not have any major complications. But ice in the engine caused the plane to spin over the Alps. It flipped over again and again, and then began a seemingly unstoppable seven-hundred-foot free fall. When the pilot finally regained control, we could see the mountaintops *above* us. The visibility was still bad, and there was little reason to believe that the pilot and I would get off the plane in one piece. Afterward we were told that we had disappeared off the radar in Milan. They had notified the company in Gütersloh, and everyone had expected the worst.

In these tense minutes, during which my fate hung by a string, I wrote a farewell letter to the woman who had become my life's companion, and whose unconditional support had meant the world to me: Liz, who is now my second wife. After many years of a close personal relationship, we married in Gütersloh in 1982 and thus sealed what had begun in 1957, when we first met at a Bertelsmann company party. It had lasted for so many years.

Like so many young people of my generation, I had married young right after the war and started a family. People change, and within a few years, my first wife and I separated. I have always enjoyed my contact with my children, Johannes, Susanne, and Christiane, but given the fact that I was a passionate entrepreneur, the time I had to spend with my family was limited.

My second wife, Liz, had started working at Bertelsmann at a very young age. In all those years, she never once avoided challenges; she mastered all her difficult tasks very well. We got along well in our business life and in our personal life. To me she was and always will be a wonderful completion to my life. I had the experience in leadership, while Liz exhibited excellent skills for evaluating and motivating employees and managers. Our personalities complemented each other, both privately and with regard to corporate objectives. Many evenings were spent discussing our daily experiences and the possible further development of the Bertelsmann corporate culture.

A few years back, my wife took on important functions within the Bertelsmann Foundation and within the Bertelsmann AG. Her good judge of character has made her an important leader of our company. Her obvious enjoyment of personal contact with people has led her to worldwide connections with scientists, economic leaders, and politicians. I trust that the continuity of our corporation will be in good hands with her. Her personal involvement, which reaches far beyond entrepreneurial issues to my children and grandchildren, fills me with joy and gratitude. Liz always tries to give talented young people a chance, and she knows from her own experiences how important motivation and compassion can be for the first steps in a career.

Of the three children we had together—Christoph, Brigitte, and Andreas—our daughter worried us most. Brigitte suffered from many bouts of severe pneumonia, and we often feared for her life, which, of course, put Liz and me under extreme stress. Every winter Liz and our daughter would travel to southern countries, but even so, breakdowns could not always be avoided. In our desperation, we faced the calloused advice of doctors: "Let the child die!" But my wife never gave up. Her undying devotion and commitment saved our daughter's life.

Brigitte later studied in the United States in order to collect international experiences. She now holds a leadership position at the Stroke Initiative that my wife started, continuing to develop a network throughout the world to fight stroke. Within our country and in cooperation with several foreign countries, the work of the German Stroke Initiative saved thousands of lives. While our son Christoph distinguishes himself with great independence, Brigitte, in her own goal-oriented and responsible way, shares my opinion that everyone has to give back to society. As a member of the board at the foundation, she does her share to maintain the continuity of the Bertelsmann Foundation.

THE DIALOGUE OF CULTURES: A NECESSITY FOR GLOBAL COEXISTENCE

During my tenure as chairman of the board of the Bertelsmann Foundation, Liz and I traveled abroad many times.

We wanted to discover exemplary initiatives overseas and bring them back for utilization in Germany, as well as present model projects the foundation had tested in Germany and make them available to other countries.

The heart of our efforts was always to initiate a dialogue above and beyond purely national interests and cultural differences. Often our involvement in one country would pique the interest of another country, and over the years many international building blocks fell into place. In 1991, for example, the Bertelsmann Foundation held a conference in Barcelona, in which we discussed the international objectives of our corporation in general and our objectives in the Mediterranean in particular. We presented the foundation's fields of activity and discussed our particular involvement in education before an audience of many politicians and press. One example was the foundation of a school of journalism in Jerusalem, which I had initiated and developed with my friend Teddy Kollek, then mayor of Jerusalem.

At the end of the conference, two journalists from Egypt approached me, asking about the possibilities of educational support in their home country. Their approach led to an idea for an educational project in Egypt. Despite Egypt's historical significance and its impressive historic structures, much of the country outside its cities is impoverished and offers little educational opportunities. During our initial contact with the president's wife, Suzanne Mubarak, we noticed a common ground with regard to educational ideas. During our very first conversation, we decided to systematically develop the Egyptian library system and to make it a fore-most educational tool. We knew this project could benefit greatly from our experiences with the reconceptualizing of public libraries all over Germany (and particularly in my hometown, Gütersloh). We aimed to develop a network of libraries all across Egypt, as well as to institute a systematic training program for librarians.

For many years we worked closely with Mrs. Mubarak and the Egyptian educational institutions. To foster the project, my wife and I went to Cairo at least thirty times during that period. I have fond recollections of our friends and our work there. Current cross-border developments in Europe illustrate how difficult it can be to peacefully inte-grate cultures that have developed independently over thou-sands of years. Our Egyptian example has shown us that patience, involvement, and friendships are indispensable tools in the promotion of peace and the fueling of progress in the world.

I feel a strong connection with the Middle East. Initiated by my friend and business partner Oscar Dystel and by Teddy Kollek, the foundation worked on several projects in Israel. In 2003, my wife and I were honored with the Teddy Kollek Award for our efforts there. This award, which carries my old friend's name, has brought me great joy.

For decades the political arm of the Bertelsmann Founda-tion focused on ways in which to secure peace in a world of vastly different political systems and expansive national interests. In my dialogue with political, economic, and scientific leaders, I have repeatedly pointed out that the vicious cycle of military might does not guarantee peace, but rather begets ever new wars and territorial destruction.

After all, the idea of a unified Europe lived for centuries only in the imagination of philosophers and humanitarian writers, who, like the French author Victor Hugo, envisioned a "United States of Europe."[2] The European idea seemed altogether elusive, especially after the enormous destruction of two world wars. And yet, German Chancellor Konrad Adenauer, English Prime Minister Winston Churchill, French Secretary of State Robert Schuman, and Italian government official Alcide de Gasperi managed to create the basis and international contractual premises that would eventually guarantee the rule of law and equal rights among the Western European nations. In the end it was the recognition of our common economic interests that led to the breakthrough for our mutual international cooperation. The European Coal and Steel Community, founded in 1951, was the first milestone in the reconciliation process among former enemies. But even today the European nations' pathway toward a sustainable community of nations is fraught with difficulty. The expansion brought about by the fall of the Berlin Wall in 1989 and the breakdown of the Soviet Union in 1991, when the Eastern European nations lined up for membership, has brought with it new challenges. The current debate over membership for Turkey and Croatia reveals deep-seated cultural differences within the European continent and points to the extensive efforts that will be required if we wish to instigate forms of true cooperation that place common goals and responsibilities above national interests.

The European Union was founded to foster lasting peace in the heart of Europe, yet its growth and successes are the result of the economic activities of the Union, both internally and internationally. The European Union can achieve its political objective of peace only by securing its economic competitiveness. The extraordinary complexity of the European societies and the ever-growing demands on progress and quality of life have been widening the gap between rich and poor. This abyss presents an enormous challenge for the European community of nations that can only be managed with a high degree of competence and efficiency. Leadership techniques that can make democracies internationally competitive will play a significant role. We cannot participate in a cultural dialogue and work toward sociopolitical and economic cooperation if we cling to an attitude of Western superiority. We have to respect different historical perspectives and be open toward other ways of life. The political system of a modern democracy has to be persuasive, and it can only be persuasive if it is able to satisfy people's demands for progress and development.

The experiences of the Bertelsmann Corporation during its early phase of internationalization, and the international experiences of the Bertelsmann Foundation, have taught me that the immediate dialogue and cooperation toward common economic and social goals can be a successful means of overcoming borders and improving cultural communication problems. The people of the world understand more and more that military means, which threaten human existence, are no alternative to true political efforts.

History has shown that power and violence can neither maintain nor sustain human order. Spiritual orientation is a vital ingredient as well. In the end, it is the values and rules of a culture that decide which political order will prevail. If we want to initiate political and social reform, we also have to discuss the spiritual orientation of a nation or a community of nations. A continuous dialogue about common cultural values above and beyond national, religious, and political borders must be among our first and foremost efforts! Only if the members of a community share common values and goals will they commit to its development and feel motivated to get personally involved. And just as democracy cannot simply claim superiority due to its historical victories, churches cannot simply define their message based on a historical claim, either. Regardless of whether we are dealing with the cultural characteristics of communities, political systems of nations, or the spiritual orientation of humans, the changing power of time influences them all. Nothing stays the way it is. No dogma will withstand the challenges of time.

THE CONTINUITY OF DEMOCRACY
AND LEADERSHIP

The system of democracy as a social order, in which an elected government represents the political will of the people, has its origin in antiquity. The citizens of Athens knew their politicians personally and held opinions about them. This made a direct connection with the democratic leadership possible, for they in turn knew, from their own experience, the living conditions of the people. This mutual transparency not only released great potential and allowed for the delegation of responsibility to individual citizens. It also ensured that the progress-oriented Greek society was defined freely, taking into account the input of each individual citizen.

The claim to power has undergone many transformations over the millennia, and through these years has received its justification by way of territorial possession, military might, knowledge, or spiritual foundation. In modern times, national states and cultures that are based on hierarchical and totalitarian systems face off with democratic states, where the citizens' votes carry weight.

Yet the ideal of a national state is fragile above and beyond its various sociopolitical manifestations. Wars and national conflicts have shown that a political order based on cultures and national boundaries can barely do justice to global developments. While the nation-state structure still dominates the world, conflicts between different cultures

are becoming more and more apparent: Muslim and funda-
mentalist values clash with those of the Christian West. The
Cold War rivalry of the superpowers has been supplanted
by a multitude of cultural and ethnic conflicts.[3]

Religious and philosophical beliefs, along with basic
values, social relations, social customs, and even worldviews, can vary greatly within these cultures. Global policies
cannot withdraw from these multipolar and multicultural
challenges. The economic success of Asia is rooted in Asian
culture. Likewise, the difficulties of developing democracies
in Asia are rooted in Asian culture as well. Within the Islamic culture there are many issues that hinder both democratic and economic development.[4]

Due to a global exchange of information and fast techno-
logical and scientific developments, which were unimaginable only a few years ago, people all over the world can
now compare their own way of life with that of other people
and cultures. Such comparisons intensify demands for the
improvement of one's own living standards, and may even
lead to cultural and social conflicts. The political order and
the actions of the ruling class face faster and more resolute
criticism.

The speed of economic change in India and China, as
well as the rapid economic development in Arabic states and
in the former Soviet Union, show us that democracy and
economic growth are no longer the only possible alliance
that leads to progress and competitiveness.

Many politicians in Germany believe that they hold in

their hands a patent system of order that is inviolable and permanent, all due to the historical justification of democracy as a successful form of state. Only slowly do we recognize that in the era of change even democracy as a state form needs constant renewal. Analyzing the need for reform and how to attain it is among the most important tasks of democratic action.[5] People only identify with the political and cultural achievements of their community if they understand the motivation behind their community's objectives and are willing to personally support them.

For democracy to compete successfully against other political systems, it must continually persuade, even in this, the era of global change!

Our democratic leadership must critically look at our political systems, our social objectives, and our spiritual orientation in a way that their successes can be measured and evaluated. Measuring and evaluating success and performance requires the comparison of political and social action data from other countries and democratic orders. We need standards that measure efficiency and effectiveness. Modern information techniques offer many such opportunities for comparison.

The success of a modern democracy is significant for the motivation of its citizens. It influences citizens' faith in the policies of their country. A loss of faith in politics can only be counteracted with a transparency of the standard of political action. Voters need to be taken seriously as mature citizens. This is only possible if the standard of political action is read in measurable ways, because only then can mature citizens effectively evaluate success or failure of their government. A comparison of performance, particularly in the exclusive domains of the state—education, administration, and state finance—can reveal shocking deficits. Motivated and responsible citizens do not grow on trees. They have to be persuaded with political action!

Change begins at the top, even if it concerns societal goals and operative patterns. Just like our economic leaders, so our politicians and state officials must recognize that a worldwide comparison of their performance will create competition. Whether we win or lose depends as much on our ideas and objectives as it does on the competence of our leaders.

There is no way around it: The competition of political systems has begun with all its might, and can only be won with strength and courage for progress. We still have a way to go before we can set an example. But we can utilize encouraging examples from other countries if we compare global variants of democratic order with an eye on their performance.

The immigrant mentality of the Anglo-Saxon society, which gave me as a young man so many ideas, can still be of help to us today by demanding "as little government as possible, and more responsibility to the citizen." If we wish to follow this example, we need an additional principle that, as entrepreneurial experience shows, fosters the individual's sense of responsibility and motivates individual involvement: the delegation of responsibility. The hierarchical structures inherent in an authoritarian state cannot possibly reach its citizenry. A successful democracy must maintain a constant dialogue with its citizens and thereby guarantee the continuous revision of its strategic planning and action. This is the only way that our democracy can satisfy the people's demand for progress. The experience of the last few decades has shown us that democracy is able to compete. But just as in the economic arena, reform starts at the top. These dearly needed reforms in state, administration, and politics need to be carried by the citizens. We are dealing with *their* state; the future is in *their* hands! Those who know the power of competition must understand that our success or failure in the global world order is in our hands.

Allow me to note from the perspective of my decades of experiences as an entrepreneur that economic success and progress are measured by competition. Product improvements generated by the free-market economy have led to an unimaginable improvement in the living conditions of many countries around the globe. Progress can be promoted by competition.

By contrast, such forces are rare within the democratic system. Our state still makes decisions in an authoritarian way based on political calculation. Efficiency is not a standard that governs action. This raises the question of whether the goals and methods of state action are even valid in the era of global competition. The power of political influence, as well as the decision-making process, still lies with nation-states, although the leadership of these countries is under growing siege by external groups and global capital markets.

The most recent financial crisis and the escalating prices for raw materials have shown the helplessness of national states when facing global risks. National policies of "distribution" are unrealistic in the global market. New ways and means are key! As is done in the area of military security politics, international experts in performance-oriented leadership techniques should exchange ideas with forward-thinking politicians in order to develop strategies that can meet the global demands and challenges of political effectiveness.

EXPERIENCES WITH OUR CORPORATE CULTURE

My experiences with the Bertelsmann corporate culture have shown me that the singular orientation toward capital growth as the determining benchmark of success will ultimately lead nowhere. Corporate performance depends on more than the bottom line. Managerial motivation and commitment to the corporation are significant values, which can have a strong influence on the successful growth and continuity of a company.

In my decades as entrepreneur, the following basic tenets have been consistently valuable:

1. A corporate culture that relies on motivation is in many ways superior to a traditional hierarchical leadership style.

2. Management behavior based on fairness and compassion reduces social differences and fosters motivation.

3. The following principles can improve any basic contract:

    a. *more individual freedom along with the delegation of responsibility;*

    b. *profit sharing as a means to increase employee commitment to the corporation;*

    c. *a health plan as a means to greatly increase motivation;*

    d. *ongoing cooperation with the company union representatives above and beyond immediate problem solving;*

    e. *employee commitment to the corporation as a means to visibly increase corporate performance and willingness for innovation;*

    f. *easier capital procurement in a company thus defined.*

Aligning the interests of employees and entrepreneur by means of a corporate culture defined by cooperation can set an example for the political demand that the economic world be guided by compassion and fairness. The political leadership must use techniques that follow the standard of a corporate culture seeking to supersede traditional capitalism with more efficient forms of creative and flexible partnerships. It could be highly advantageous for the state and society to give its citizenry good cause to align with and commit to the conditions and opportunities of democratic action. For our market is by now a global market!

For more than fifty years our democracy has juggled the interests of employees and entrepreneurs by way of unions and management. Entrepreneurs are represented by management associations; and workers and employees, by unions. The form and tone of employer/employee negotiations have developed into a partisan system, and are often conducted in a combative manner. "Lockouts" and "strikes" are popular instruments of these processes that, unlike in political discussions, don't lead merely to a definition of viewpoint and party line, but rather to actual fiscal consequences. This can potentially lead to prolonged ill will between the parties involved.

The arguments between the opponents may be so serious that they accuse each other of ulterior motives. Such accusations can linger even after an agreement is reached and lead to a demotivation, which in turn can negatively influence the corporate atmosphere. During a combative exchange, the entrepreneur no longer sets an example, and the consequences of inappropriate managerial behavior can have prolonged negative effects on the reform processes necessary to ensure competitiveness in the global marketplace.

Furthermore, the damage done to the national economy can be extraordinarily significant, though it has never been historically analyzed. In a time of global competition, this becomes even more important. The negative effect of combative arguments on the national economy can be a lasting slowdown of economic growth. Therefore, this form of conflict resolution cannot be considered a forward-looking instrument for efficient economic policies or corporate management. In light of the global market, we need to strive for solutions that create less friction and rather equate a balance of interests in a democratic model of cooperation. If open-minded entrepreneurs can transfer the motivation and commitment needed for their own work to their managers and employees, the system can change for the better.

Transparence and cooperation release unimaginable energies, because respectful cooperation can define common goals more sharply, and then recognize and remove unnecessary barriers more quickly.

Cooperation based on partnership that has been tested in an entrepreneurial culture, which strives for common goals regarding capital distribution and develops social services for the common good (rather than fostering disagreements among employers and employees regarding wealth distribution), can be a model for global political challenges as well. In the years of Bertelsmann's development, I have noticed over and over again that our corporate culture is successful because it offers advantages to everyone involved:

1. Capital receives a higher return because of the motivation and engagement of all those involved.

2. Investors and management have better opportunities and a higher success rate because all involved show the willingness to cooperate. The delegation of responsibility increases the freedom of good leadership personnel.

3. Managers have much influence on the success rate. Yet they also must set an example in their performance and behavior. Leadership personnel should know from history that every culture needs a spiritual orientation. Ethics are vital for any successful community. This is true for corporate success as well.

Anyone who considers the refinement of our democratic ideals an important task should not do without the cooperation of motivated and involved citizens. Only those who can align the social needs and individual interests of the people with the democratic goals of a society can achieve the objectives of the future. For a long time employees had little impact in the economic realm; and citizens had little influence on the state. The political world can learn from entrepreneurial experience. The following insights are key:

1. The quality of leadership within political debate should be measured by international cooperation rather than disagreement. The political leadership should work toward exchanging combative disagreements with attempts at partnership and cooperation.

2. Corporate constitutions must adjust to the conditions of the global economy. The tools that enable a corporation and union representatives to cooperate on such issues as information, advice, and dialogue need to be strengthened. The first and foremost task of the union representatives should no longer be able to engage in combative disagreements but to help maintain a just, human, and successful corporate culture. Profit sharing is part of that as well!

Regardless of whether we are discussing a corporation or a country, people know best from their own experiences what needs improvement. Yet good suggestions will dry up if they continually fall on deaf ears within the management or administration. If, however, employees can commit to the goals of their corporation due to profit sharing or other means, involvement will seem natural, because their action affects them personally.

The tenets that have been successful within a globally active corporation cannot be ignored for the development of a globally active democratic culture: We need motivated citizens who are willing to get personally involved because they are committed to the goals of their communities.

THE SIGNIFICANCE OF DEMOCRATIC PRINCIPLES FOR A COOPERATION OF CULTURES

The educational and consumer goods that people want and need these days are distributed unevenly throughout the world. Certain goods, such as food and medication, are subsistence goods, while others may be desirable but not necessary. The evaluation of these categories depends in part upon culture and varies greatly in different regions, despite a dominance of the Western industrial culture.

Yet despite all cultural differences, people everywhere strive for an improvement of their living standard, and ultimately desire a life of dignity and freedom.

Personal freedom of the individual depends not only on the political system but also on the economic promise of one's profession. People work hard for the conditions they consider to be prerequisites for a happy life. All over the world wealth is seen as proof of personal achievements and is too often confused with happiness. In the economic realm, while it is unreasonable to expect the same performance from everyone, it is possible to expect the same effort from everyone. This basic idea matters in all communities. The challenge to political leaders is to steer these efforts according to our times. No matter how variable the economic conditions are, the demand for an international economic ethic that balances compassion with a certain standard of performance is vital.

A capitalism that disregards human needs disregards humanity and will ultimately give rise to social revolt and political conflict. Peaceful coexistence becomes impossible. The entrepreneur who makes money with his employees' work is responsible for his employees. Particularly in today's global marketplace, a responsible entrepreneur can offer path-breaking insights, because the human need for freedom, peace, and wealth is similar regardless of national, cultural, and political differences. The balance of interests can be achieved most easily if people communicate in similar ways.

We are at a crossroads. Will the next generation's fight for distribution become a "war of cultures," leading to brutal wars and revolts with international consequences?[6] Or will the experiences of our democratic systems be able to set a common course and create a consensus that enables the peaceful cooperation of different cultures?

But what would the necessary conditions be, exactly? What must we still learn to make a dialogue possible that reaches beyond ethnic and territorial borders?

The people of the world are about to understand that, due to devastating consequences, military action is no alternative to path-breaking political efforts. Politicians and economic leaders try to create a peaceful balance of interests by creating common institutions and international goals. Yet the status of these efforts is inadequate. Our future looks grim. International relations are still hindered by expansionist national endeavors and a lack of mutual trust. The responsible parties are still stuck with outdated goals and standards for success, and are thus unable to consider pioneering global solutions. The rulers of the world still think that the mightiest will win!

But as long as might and size are what defines success, peaceful cooperation among peoples and cultures will remain a goal of the distant future.

How many more wars do we need to understand that the political distinction of cultures and nations is not tenable? People have to experience that their interests are no longer secured in national units, nor in their fight for political and economic dominance. Our times demand a consolidation of efforts to survive the global struggle for survival.

But if we wish to secure peace and compassion in this global development, we must find an internationally workable order that is based on ethical goals and compassionate action. This order must align an individual's right to dignity and self-determination with the goals of the community, and therefore continuously refine the political process. *Pante rhei*—all is in flux, and no person nor power of the world can suspend the law of constant change! Totalitarian systems and hierarchical political orders tend to be arrogant and fall for the falsity that they can transfer their own political system to other states. Yet the rapid exchange of information in the global era, which permits constant comparisons of lifestyles and educational opportunities via the Internet, can reveal willfulness and the abuse of power. There is justified hope that political constructs carried by one-sided interests will eventually fail, if people can see themselves as global citizens.

If people want to survive, they must show the insight and courage to support the political order that can best do justice to the need for compassion and freedom: The political system of democracy is the only form that allows people to impact their own future. Although it is fraught with faults and needs refinement and completion (just like everything else that is man-made), there is no real alternative to the democratic political order. If we want to convince other cultures and political orders that democracy is the way of the future, then it is entirely up to us, the citizens of the Western democracies, to ascertain, refine, and support the sociopolitical opportunities in our lives. Persuading is not self-righteousness! An effective role model is far more persuasive: a compassionate, peaceful, and economically successful community, which engages in a trustworthy dialogue that seeks cooperation and consensus, and which offers representatives of different cultures the chance to incorporate their experiences in the political process.

There is no doubt that one of the most difficult political tasks is to revise and develop social systems. A hierarchical understanding of politics cannot manage that. We are at the beginning of a learning curve with still equal amounts of opportunities and dangers. But fear, justified or not, should never tempt us to support solutions that do not serve human nature. Where people meet, conflicts of interest are unavoidable. But it is up to us to decide whether conflicts turn into fights, whether bridges are built, or gaps are widened, separating us further from other cultures.

But how can we find a balance between opposing political systems and differing cultures and their goals? The only possible way is open communication: We need to "get to know each other" and "talk with each other." That is the key to international dialogue. Every individual carries partial responsibility for the success of such a dialogue. The citizens of democratic countries should know that their vote counts! Everybody needs to contribute their own share and develop alternatives based on their own conscience and their personal knowledge, alternatives that can channel human egoism and hunger for power. We need an analytical comparison of democracies and a transparent communication of possible solutions for the many challenges and open questions that accompany any social progress. Without the constant effort to revise our democratic systems in cooperation with different cultures, we cannot succeed in the global fight for justice, freedom, and humanity. Spiritual orientation is indispensable in this process!

PROGRESS NEEDS SPIRITUAL ORIENTATION

Throughout history, successful dialogue between people of different backgrounds has been considered an art form, because mere communication itself sometimes harbors seemingly insurmountable difficulties. The philosophers Socrates and Plato define dialogue as an effort to reveal a hidden truth.[7] But what kind of truth are we looking for in our enlightened times? Which values of society, humanity, and liberty are universal? What role does religion play? How can a dialogue of world religions help secure freedom in an ever more global environment?

New studies show that despite the differences that have shaped the world religions over the millennia, there are numerous similarities that can form the basis of a peaceful future. All cultures share a notion of spirituality: lives of integrity, pursuing not only personal happiness but also the common good. According to these studies, the defining pillars of spirituality are honesty, truthfulness, responsibility, and tolerance.[8] In my experience it is these spiritual pillars that even in secular societies define an individual's relationship to his community. Therefore, these same pillars define an individual's level of commitment and his motivation to get involved. The notion of compassion embodies the respect with which we approach the foreign, the other. This respect is the basis of an intercultural and interreligious dialogue that may lead to peaceful coexistence in our global world.

Different religious convictions are inextricably bound to

differing ways of life. What matters is not so much whether one accepts another religion, but whether one accepts the way of life that accompanies it. One of the most relevant questions today is whether, in a time of constant international and intercultural migration, foreign residents should adapt to their host country or maintain their original way of life.

The exchange of political and economic interests among people of divergent religious convictions and of differing national origins harbors challenges as well. All over the world, religious communities pursue interests that are essential for the stability of their community. One of the more important questions facing us deals with the generational continuity of religious ideals and ways of life. Religious values vary greatly among Europe, Asia, Africa, and America, and it is not always the distinction between Eastern and Western ways of life, or among Muslim, Buddhist, or Judeo-Christian forms of faith, for example, that define these variations. In Europe, particularly in Germany, Christianity has lost much of its significance within only a few generations, while in the United States the enormous rebound of spirituality shows beyond a doubt that modernization does not necessarily go hand in hand with secularization.[9]

What is certainly true for all countries is that the development of religious attitudes is a result of a long social process.

The destructive effects of two world wars and two dictatorships in the heart of Europe have left marks for generations to come. Despite globalization, Islam generally aims to counteract any trend toward secularization and individualization of religious ideas and practices, and rather imposes commitment to traditional notions of Islam. Just as with all world religions, there are many different manifestations of Islam, with divergent religious ideals and practices. Considering the distinction between numerous religious groups within Islam, which for Western communities is most clear in the conflict between Sunnites and Shiites, questions of religious authority and infallibility of the Holy Scriptures and their legal norms are rather significant, stirring up political and religious conflict.

These days, relevant news travels fast to people all over the world, regardless of religious conviction, national borders, and cultural distinctions. More than ever before, people can compare their own situation with the personal and social conditions in other cultures and countries. This can create ever-more-urgent demands for improved living conditions. People can see the whole world. Some leaders therefore feel that they have to secure their power by sheer force and territorial aggression. Some countries are in immense danger of being drawn into dangerous global conflicts. Political systems that are defined only by national or cultural considerations cannot handle that. What was unthinkable in the past needs to be considered today: Humankind must find a universal system of order that can avoid unwanted and dangerous global developments!

Opportunity and danger are ever-close relatives. There

are many political unknowns. Therefore, I feel the search for alternatives is even more important today. Is there a spiritual orientation that could channel these diverse and different objectives? The time when alarming international developments force political action is no longer in the distant future. How will our democracies react? Will they be able to create believable and workable alternatives for international coexistence? What role can the indispensable power of a strong spiritual orientation play? What are the common values upon which an international, intercultural, and interreligious exchange could take place to seek a universally binding spiritual orientation?

There are those who will think these considerations utopian. But it is no coincidence that Pope Benedict XVI has revived the interreligious dialogue. The exchange between Christians and Muslims has become more powerful and binding.[10] The debate focuses on the relationship between faith and reason, religion and violence. These efforts of our religious leaders to approach one another in such a fundamental way must not be dismissed. Each and every meeting, each and every signed declaration, is a milestone on the long road to global coexistence.

For the skeptics, remember Helsinki, 1975. At the time, Communist leaders signed a charter defining religious freedom. This was the first common declaration of personal individual freedom in Eastern and Western Europe, and it set in motion more than we could ever imagine at the time. The historically proven power of spiritual orientation should give us courage and strength in our efforts to find alternatives! It is precisely this combination—spiritual orientation and democracy—that can withstand the dangers of authoritarianism. The urgency of such initiatives in a time of nuclear threat should be obvious.

CORPORATE CULTURE AND DEMOCRACY: OUR HOPES FOR THE FUTURE

There were many mistakes and misfirings during Bertelsmann's journey to success. But as Roman thinker Marcus Aurelius said, only those who have the courage to act will achieve their goals. His credo was: "A wrongdoer is often a man who has left some thing undone, not always one who has done something."[11] Growth always takes place in dangerous waters; change and transformation do not come without risk.

This is precisely why I ask myself whether my belief in the power of economic and democratic freedom can offer a basis for peaceful coexistence in a global world. In the years of National Socialism, as a student, officer, and POW, I have experienced the dark side of hierarchical leadership techniques and all their gruesome effects on Europe, Africa, and America. It is clear to me: Violence and force cannot be the premise of a successful order. Compassion and exemplary behavior are the indispensable tools of a successful leader.

After World War II, my being asked to take responsibility for Bertelsmann was a great opportunity—and a huge challenge. I have never regretted my decision to take this chance and face the challenge head-on. The opportunity to be an international entrepreneur and to build an international corporation in cooperation with different cultures is the most exciting duty I can imagine.

My personal convictions led me to begin the process of reform in the early years: I implemented fairness and compassion as the pillars of the Bertelsmann corporation. Along the way I met with many skeptics and pessimists who did not believe that an entrepreneurial culture was relevant. There's no doubt that my opinions were rather controversial at first. Could anyone really believe that an entrepreneur could behave compassionately, respectfully, and fairly? Many representatives of public opinion, numerous politicians, members of the business world, and journalists reacted with doubts. Even today many are skeptical about my ideas that the pillars of entrepreneurial culture might harbor the pillars for global coexistence.

And so, looking back on the highs and lows of my long journey, I wonder, Is my unconditional belief in the power of the entrepreneurial culture a dream from which we will awaken once capitalism has been set free upon the world? Or will the analysis of my life's work show that the relation of human freedom and economic and political development is truly significant and will allow us to view the future with a hopeful eye?

I still ponder these questions; even today I ruminate over situations and decisions made on this, my entrepreneurial journey. And those in my hometown Gütersloh greet this long-distance walker with a smile, still, as he continues on his way, as he has done for decades, during all seasons, come rain or shine.

Positive development requires that we ponder critical questions, and that is why I made sure that my thesis of the relationship between a well-developed entrepreneurial culture and the economic success of a corporation was tested time and again. A well-planned research project of the Bertelsmann companies found significant common characteristics that could illustrate the effectiveness of the entrepreneurial culture.[12] The results of this study can be summarized as follows:

1. Bertelsmann companies with a well-developed entrepreneurial culture are more successful economically than Bertelsmann companies that do not yet show much of a cooperative character.

2. There is a clear relation between employee commitment and economic success. The companies that are most successful economically are the companies that show a high degree of satisfaction with the managerial qualities of cooperation and commitment.

3. A high degree of employee commitment fosters more productive behavior and better health among employees. The number of resignations, sick days,

and extended periods of illness are directly related to employee commitment.

4. Employee motivation is directly influenced by the degree of cooperation of direct supervisors and corporate management. A structural comparison revealed that cooperation directly influences employee commitment. The relation has been constant over many years and in many different cultures, as has been revealed in employee questionnaires.

These results support my idea that a cooperative leadership philosophy is relevant, and they support our desire to further develop the Bertelsmann corporate culture in the future.

Knowing the economic power of a deeply democratic behavior that places the individual in the center of debate and uses cooperation as its standard of leadership can change our future! If people from many different cultural backgrounds take their lead for personal motivation and commitment from a cooperative leadership style, we will have made a significant step toward a cooperative global world. People of different cultural heritages can march into our future together.

In a time of global commerce and information flow, people all over the world expect progress in their personal living conditions and their social order, tending more toward peace and justice. It is high time that we leave behind the purely combative stance on our national and international levels and start striving for a common idea of man. The power of spiritual orientation is indispensable. The current discussion about national sovereignty must also deal with the notion of global responsibility in the face of catastrophes such as floods or earthquakes (as recently experienced in Asia). This is a responsibility we cannot hide from now, not when images of catastrophes inundate the world.

Throughout history Human Rights have been hard-won. The first Declaration of Human Rights in 1948 was preceded by endless debates. The fact that different cultures have different ideas about what constitutes Human Rights should not prevent us from looking toward a cooperative future. People all over the world want to improve their living conditions. If we are serious about the ethics of global cooperation, we must both accept responsibility for and support cooperative systems that focus on compassion and fairness. While the desire for power leads to injustice and combat, the relation of economic performance and compassionate leadership will find support all over the world. Violence and arrogance are no alternatives.

Global competition will show that Western capitalism can only be successful if it accepts and fosters the pillars of humanity. The Bertelsmann Corporation has shown that.

The long-denied significance of personal motivation and individual commitment are our great untapped reserves of strength that will lead us into the future.

I am full of optimism that we will succeed in utilizing this potential for global cooperation. And I am determined to walk this path to the very end. My unconditional belief in compassion and cooperation was no dream. It is the experience of my lifetime.

HOMEWORK ESSAY OF THE STUDENT REINHARD MOHN

Fall 1937 to January 5, 1938

MY THOUGHTS ON CHOOSING
A PROFESSION

It has not been that long since someone told me that one's life begins the moment we finally accept our tasks and responsibilities, and start fulfilling them. "Another one of those moral dogmas," I thought at first, and never heard a single word that followed. Talking about tasks and responsibilities didn't resonate with me. On the one hand this may be because we are forced to hear such standard, well-meaning phrases several times a day. On the other hand, I also believed that nobody had the right to criticize me; I was convinced that I fulfilled all my duties at school and elsewhere. And then to tell me that I needed a goal—I was sure that I was doing fine in that regard as well. Thus far I had thought that my job was to do well in school, and that my goal was to finish high school with a good grade-point average.

When I heard that life begins when you start working toward a goal and try to do your duty, I felt I was well on my way to doing just that, especially considering that I had already decided upon a goal and did my best to comply with everything that was asked of me as diligently as possible. So I wasn't concerned. Within a few hours I had forgotten all about it. Just a few weeks later I heard how some of my friends were talking about their future and their profession. I didn't think much about it, as I believed that there was plenty of time to choose a profession, and I didn't want to worry about it yet. But then I remembered the earlier conversation, and I suddenly realized that a high school diploma could not be my final goal. My final goal had to be bigger and go further. My work could not be done just by finishing school; that would be just the beginning! The high school diploma therefore was not an end in itself, it was a beginning; and the work at school not a task as such, but the preparation for my true task. These new thoughts shattered everything that had so far guided me and given my work meaning. I was forced to set a new goal; for you cannot enjoy and appreciate your work if you do not know what you are working for.

But I had so many questions and doubts that I didn't know what was true, nor which way to turn. Sometimes

I tried to forget everything new and to go back to what seemed tried-and-true to me. But these thoughts would come back over and over again, and with them came a sense of uneasiness. Was it joy, or was it fear? Fear of being alone, of not knowing what my future would bring? Because I knew that soon my parents couldn't take care of me anymore. Everything they did for me and that I took for granted I would soon have to do myself. Or was it the joy of having that responsibility? I wouldn't depend on others anymore and could do whatever I wanted without asking for permission. I would no longer be a burden to anyone, but make a living on my own. All these questions culminated in one question: the question of my goal and my profession.

I was thinking about different professions, but I could never quite decide for any one in particular. Sometimes I thought I would find a particularly fitting and interesting task in this area, and other times I thought something else might be even more suitable. I kept on searching like that for a long time, until I realized that first and foremost I had to decide which standards were important in my life, my work, and my future. I found three things that seemed particularly important for one's choice of profession. They are: responsibility toward the community, talent and the desire for personal freedom, and a spiritual life. The first became clear to me when I wondered why people worked, and where this work was supposed to take us. These thoughts can come easily these days. Technology and economy hurry along in huge strides. People invent, build, try, and then improve, and improve again. Why all this work? Where is it all supposed to lead us? What is the end of all this? Despite all our knowledge, we will never find the answer to this question. This is the border we cannot cross no matter how hard we think; this is where reason meets faith and religion. It is impossible to keep questioning ourselves this way until we find the answer, for our reason will never lead us to a final answer. It is important to form an opinion in these matters, but this should not lead to the notion that there is an answer we can find by reason. Therefore, I do not want to ponder these questions. Instead, I want to set and deal with standards that hold me accountable in my work. For I believe that I did not get my life and my strength to use it wherever I want to; I believe that there is a power beyond me that will direct and control me. This power is my people, my community. I share responsibility for its welfare. The community guarantees law and order within the state, which in turn enables our work. In turn, every individual needs to fulfill a duty with all the strength and effort at our disposal. This demands that we choose our profession responsibly. For if we are to use all our strength at work, the way we are supposed to, we need to have a profession that actually allows us to do so. It is unlikely that we would ever choose a profession for which we lack the physical or intellectual requirements. A cerebral person will not think of becoming a handyman; nor will someone who has a hard time with intellectual work choose a profession in the sciences. I think the danger lies elsewhere: It is the danger that we choose a profession out of convenience, a profession that will not demand from us what we could otherwise deliver. Of course it is possible to spend eight hours or more a day in such a profession and fill up one's days. But such a profession will not offer true satisfaction. At least it cannot offer satisfaction to those who are aware of and try to fulfill their duties toward their people. Convenience and a cowardly flight from our duties to the community are not only great dangers now that I am deciding upon my profession, but they will be dangers for the rest of my life. For there will be many forks in my road that will lead me away from the goal I have set for myself. My goal is to perform as well as I possibly can. I have not yet chosen a specific goal to pursue. I just want to work with others and do my duty in my community, which in turn will show me my destination, the goal of my work.

The second thing that will help me decide on my profession is talent. The reason that this needs to be considered I have already explained. If I mention predisposition yet again, it is because it also has another significance for my professional choice. Considering one's predisposition ought to keep me from making irrational, rash, and dangerous decisions. We are easily distracted by seemingly fantastic offers—be they a respected position or a well-compensated profession. But we may make decisions we later regret. Not everyone will feel this way. I could even imagine the opposite: that we end up being content with our choice of profession. Yet when the power that reckons with us is based not only on the externals, we may realize that we have been betrayed, and that we, in fact, have betrayed ourselves. For if we are asked to judge—if we are pushed in certain directions by others, and if we are influenced by others' opinions—we may not make fair decisions. This is certainly true when choosing our profession. Except that it is not strange voices that influence us, but it is our own voice that wants to silence our own conscience. Behind this voice stand cowardliness and selfishness. I have to be careful and only listen to my own conscience that tells me: "Your God-given talent needs to determine your profession." This is the second thing I want to consider.

As my final criterion I have listed personal freedom and spiritual life. Those in our class who focus on languages often complain about those of us who focus on mathematics that we have been petrified in formulas and equations, thinking only about mathematics and the other natural sciences, and completely disregarding the beauty of language. They say we don't know anything about the value of Greek poets and have no idea what a good poem or another work can offer. We are still laughing about such complaints, because we know them well, and we know that they don't know that much more about these matters than we do. Today we are laughing; but what will we do later? For I cannot deny that what they complain about in jest today may be true tomorrow—we may very well be blinded. I also believe that those whose profession will most likely be technical are particularly vulnerable to the danger of petrification. Now the question arises: In choosing our profession, how much guidance should we place on our desire to not freeze up, to not die inside? On the one hand you could imagine that those who think of nothing but their work will perform better than those who also take the time to read books that speak to us about the inner turmoil of man. Or that those who think of nothing but their work will perform better than those who think about other things as well. On the other hand, humans are not machines to calculate with or tools to build with as if they were made of stone. Or is this, in fact, what is necessary when we speak of duty? For the state demands all our strength and effort. Does the state therefore have the right to demand we hand over what makes us human? I cannot see the dividing line and don't yet know how I'd decide if I were faced with such a decision. In general, I believe that it is possible to combine the two (and, I think, most people do). For who would restlessly fulfill his duty and never think about himself? Who can say, "I have only done my duty in my life." Basically I believe that man embraces both; some of us are more inclined toward duty, others more toward religion and the need for a spiritual life. So I hope that thinking about this will keep me from choosing a profession that would lead to my inner petrification. For I would rather deal with all doubts and questions that come up and endlessly search for answers than become a deadened tool.

These are the thoughts that should guide my life. It is possible that much is wrong with that, and that much of it was decided in the last minute. It may also not be clear why I've chosen these three points. For I am sure that other people have to struggle with other doubts and need other guidelines. I don't want to claim that my ideas are universal. I am actually rather sure that a few years down the line I will think differently about much of this, and that I will have questions about things that seem very clear to me now. I am determined to always be open to learning and to accept what is better, even if I have to give up everything I believed thus far. Therefore, what I have written here is not meant to be a final opinion. It is rather a picture revealing my future as I see it now. It offers but a glimpse of the path I will make every effort to walk on, although I cannot yet see its final destination.

•   •   •

The thoughts you have regarding your choice of profession show that you are meeting the question that is currently most important to you with the responsibility and seriousness such a question deserves. In a clear train of thought you have mentioned the essential points that have influenced your decision. I have no doubt that you will take your later tasks as seriously as you do this decision. Realizing this about a student is perhaps one of the most joyful moments a teacher can experience. And one more joyful thing: You do honor to your class.

Very good.
Ko.
January 26, 1938

Hausaufsatz.

Meine Gedanken bei der Wahl
des Berufes.

Es ist noch nicht lange her, als mir einmal jemand sagte, man habe in Wirklichkeit nicht von dem Augenblick ab, da man erkannt habe, welche Aufgaben und Pflichten man zu erfüllen habe, und man anfange, zielbewußt auf die Erfüllung dieser Aufgaben hin zu wirken. "Wunder von den alten Moralgeschichten," dachte ich zunächst und fand auf die weiteren Worte schon gar nicht mehr hin. Im allgemeinen fühlte ich mich nämlich nicht sehr getroffen, wenn man mir meine Aufgaben und Pflichten vorhielt. Zu meiner Zeit

mag das daran liegen, daß man solche
zusammen, oder auch nur scherzhaft
gebrauchten Forderungen jeden Tag unzäh-
ligemal zu hören bekommt. Andrerseits, weil
ich glaube, daß niemand berechtigt
ist, mir solche Vorwürfe zu machen, denn
ich war davon überzeugt, daß ich meine
Pflicht in der Schule und auch sonst tat,
und wenn wir jetzt gefragt werden, was
wir für ein Ziel haben, so dachte ich, daß
bei mir auch in dieser Beziehung alles
in Ordnung sei. Bisher hatte ich nämlich
meine Aufgabe nur darin gesehen, ordentlich für die Schule zu arbeiten, und als
Abschluß und Ziel hatte ich mir vorgenommen, ein möglichst gutes Abitur zu bauen.

Als ich also nun fühle, daß man in Wirklichkeit nicht habe, wenn man auch ein Ziel
hinarbeite, und sich bemühe, seine Pflicht
zu tun, glaubte ich, daß ich denn zu
auch dann besten Wege sei, und zu erfüllen, denn ich hatte mir ja ein Ziel
gesetzt und hatte mich auch bemüht alles,
was man von mir erwartete, möglichst
gewissenhaft und ordentlich zu tun. So
bekümmerte ich mich nicht weiter und
hatte nach ein paar Stunden die ganze
Geschichte schon wieder vergessen. Einige
Wochen später fühle ich zufällig, wie meine zu meiner Kammeraden über ihre Zukunft und ihren Beruf sprechen. Ich suche
nicht lange weiter nach und meinte,

es hin zu noch einige Zeit, bis man sich
nach einem Buch umsehen müßte. Daß ich
mir jetzt lieber noch keine Kopfschmerzen
darüber machen wollen. Doch da müßte ich
plötzlich wieder an das höhere Geheimnis
denken, und wie kam mir einmal der
Gedanke, daß die Reifeprüfung gar nicht
mein letztes Ziel sein kann, sondern daß
etwas viel größeres und weiter sein müßte.
Denn wenn ich in wenigen Jahren das Abitur
machen würde, wäre ich da noch nicht am
Ende meiner Arbeit, vielmehr sollte sie
dann zu noch beginnen. Das Abitur war also
in Wirklichkeit für mich gar kein Abschluß,
sondern Anfang, und das Arbeiten für
die Schule nicht Aufgabe, sondern Vorberei-

...ting für meinen wirklichen, späteren Aufgaben, da meinen Gedanken zufliegen und alles, was früher für mich Nebensache gewesen war, und was, wie den Sinn meiner Arbeit gezeigt hatte. So wurde ich gezwungen, mir ein Ziel zu setzen; denn man kann ja nicht gern und freudig arbeiten, wenn man nicht einmal weiß, wozu man es tut.

Jetzt standen aber zweierlei Sorgen und Zweifel vor mir auf, daß ich nicht wüßte was wirklich recht sei, und wie den rechten Weg zeigen könne. Manchmal fuhr ich versucht, alles Deine wieder zu vergessen, und mich wieder um das zu halten, was für mich früher als richtig gegolten hatte.

Aber diese Gedanken kamen doch wieder, und mit ihnen kam immer ein unheimliches, beunruhigendes Gefühl. Aber die Angst, aber was es immer? Angst vor dem Alleinsein, vor der Ungewißheit über meine Zukunft? Denn ich wußte wohl, daß meine Eltern bald nicht mehr für mich sorgen können würden. Für alles, was ich von ihnen bekam, und so selbstverständlich hinnehmen, als würde es immer so bleiben, würde ich nun bald selbst sorgen müssen. Aber war es vielleicht die Furcht, gerade wegen dieser Verantwortung? Ich würde dann ja nicht mehr auf andere angewiesen sein und könnte tun, was ich wollte, ohne andere um Erlaubnis zu

fragen. Ich würde dann anderen nicht mehr
zur Last fallen, sondern selbst für meinen Lebensunterhalt sorgen. Alle diese
Gedanken drängten sich schließlich in
der einen zusammen. In der Frage
nach Ziel und Beruf.

Über die verschiedensten Berufe habe
ich nachgedacht, aber wie konnte ich mich
auch für einen bestimmten entscheiden.
Einmal glaubte ich, dass ich auf dem
Gebiet besonders schöne und interessante
Aufgaben finden würde, weil meinte
ich, passt sie für mich noch gar nicht.
So habe ich lange gesucht, bis ich einsah, dass
ich mir vor allem Dingen nicht einmal
darüber klar werden musste, nach welchem

Richtlinien ich überhaupt meine Arbeit und
Zukunft gestalten wollte. Den Dingen sah
ich so gehorchen, die mir besonders
wichtig und maßgebend bei der Wahl des
Berufes zu sein scheinen. Diese drei sind:
Verantwortung gegenüber dem Volk, Unver-
borgung und der Wunsch nach innerer Freiheit und innerem Leben. – Auch das nächste
kann ich, als ich darüber nachdachte, wofür
wir alle im Grunde eigentlich arbeiten,
und wohin uns diese Arbeit eigentlich führen
soll. Gerade heute, in unserer Zeit, können
immer diese Gedanken leicht kommen.
Mit einigen Schritten will die Technik
und Wissenschaft vorwärts. Es wird rufen-
den, gebaut, ausgerobeit und dann in-

nur und immer wieder verbessert. Wozu
aber alle diese Arbeit? Wohin soll sie
uns bringen? Was wird das Ende die=
ses Geschehens sein? — Die werdenden Men=
schen trotz allem ihrem Wissen sind
verschen. Hier ist wohl die Grenze, wo
wir mit unserem Gedanken nicht wei=
ter können, und der fußende Abstand
von dem Glauben oder der Religion ab=
gelöst wird. Hierüber weiter nachzudenken
und dieses letzte Dunkel klären
zu wollen, ist unmöglich. Die wird
uns der Abstand zu einem andgültig
richtigen Ziel bringen. Man soll wohl
zu diesen dingen Stellung nehmen,
doch darf sich nicht dazu führen, daß

...sich vornimmt, gedankenmäßig die Lösung finden zu wollen. Deshalb will ich mich nicht länger mit diesen Gedanken aufhalten, sondern mich lieber an das halten und für das arbeiten, was von mir Rechenschaft über meine Arbeit fordern wird. Denn ich glaube, daß ich mein Leben und meine Kraft nicht bekommen habe, sie willkürlich dort einzusetzen, wo ich gerade will, sondern daß über mir eine Macht steht, die mich richten und mir befehlen kann. Diese ist das Volk, in dem ich geboren bin, und für dessen Leben auch ich die Verantwortung mit tragen muß. Das Volk und die Gemeinschaft gibt dem einzelnen Ansätze für

Ruhe und Ordnung innerhalb des Betriebes
und somit die Möglichkeit zur Arbeit überhaupt. Als Gegenleistung wird dafür von
jedem Pflichterfüllung und Einsatz seiner
ganzen Kraft gefordert. Diese Forderung
legt uns auch bereits bei der Berufswahl
eine Verantwortung auf. Denn wenn
wir auf unserem Arbeitsplatz, so wie
wir es wollen, unsere ganze Kraft ein-
setzen wollen, so ist die Vorbedingung
dafür ein solcher Beruf, der uns auch
wirklich die Möglichkeit zu solcher Arbeit
gibt. Daß man sich nicht einen Beruf wählt
zu dem man die geistigen oder körper-
lichen Kräfte nicht hat, ist wahrscheinlich.
Denn sicher wird ein begabter Mensch

… überwiegend auf dem Gedanken kommen
Handwerker zu werden wie jemand,
den das gedankenmäßige Arbeiten
scheuer füllt, sich einem wissenschaft-
lichen Beruf widmen wird. Der Gegensatz auf
diesem Gebiet ist nach meiner Meinung
ein anderer, nämlich der, daß man sich
aus Bequemlichkeit eine Arbeit wählt, deren
Aufgaben von einem nicht das fordern, was
man inter anderen Verhältnissen leisten
können würde. Man wird wahrscheinlich
auch an solcher Arbeit oft mehr von sich
Nützliches an Tage schaffen und sicher auch
so den Tag ausfüllen können. Im letz-
ten Grunde zufriedenstellen wird
ein solcher Beruf einen aber nicht.

Wenigstens wird er denn nicht zusammen-
stellen, der sich seiner Pflicht gegenüber
seinem Volk bewußt ist, und sich bemüht, ihr nachzukommen. Diese Bequemlichkeit und feige Flucht vor den Aufgaben,
die das Volk stellt, sind nicht mir jetzt,
wo ich mich zu einem Ziel entscheiden will, großen Gefahren, sondern sie
werden es auch weiter in meinem Leben
bleiben. Denn immer werden wir den
rechten Weg auch solchen abzuweisen, die
mich nicht zu dem Ziel bringen wird:
Dem, das ich mir gesetzt habe. Dieses
heißt nämlich: stark bleiben wie mir
irgend in meinem Kräften steht.
Ich habe mir nicht vorgenommen etwas

ganz bestimmtes zu leisten und habe mir
auch keinen bestimmteren Aufgaben
gestellt. Ich will nur mitarbeiten und
mich bemühen meine Pflicht zu tun
in der Gemeinschaft, die mir Ziel und
Richtung meiner Arbeit weisen wird.

Als Zweites, das meinen Brief mit
bestimmen soll, habe ich die Überzeugung
genannt. Weshalb ich euch diese berück-
sichtigen muß, habe ich bald schon im
Anfang geschrieben. Wenn ich trotzdem
noch einmal die Überzeugung erwähne,
so darum, weil sie euch noch eine andere
Bedeutung für meine Schritte hat. Denn
ihre Berücksichtigung soll mich vor einem
unüberlegten, vorschnellen und gefährlichen

...schließ bekommen. Zu leicht läßt man
sich zu von scheinbar vorteilhaften Angeboten
verlocken, sei es nun sehr angenehmen
Stellung oder ein Buch, das die Möglichkeit
gibt viel Geld zu verdienen; sich so
zu entscheiden, daß es immer später genom-
men wird. Nicht jeder wird dieses später
wegfinden. Ich kann es mir sogar das
Gegenteil gut vorstellen, nämlich daß
es sehr mit seinem Buch zu finden ist.
Wenn jedoch die Macht, die nicht nur
das Äußere sieht, ihn zur Rechenschaft
ziehen wird, wird er vollkommen, daß er
seinen Betrug zum Opfer gefallen ist, und
daß er selbst es war, der sich betrog.
Denn wenn jemand über irgendetwas

…erziehen soll, und er wird von anderen
Menschen immer wieder in einer bestimmten
Richtung gedrängt, und immer wieder wird
ihm einem Meinung vor Augen gehalten,
so wird er von einer Hand nicht mehr gemacht
werden können. Ebenso ist es bei der
Erziehung. Nur sind es hier nicht fremde
Stimmen, die einen beeinflussen wollen,
sondern es ist die eigene Stimme, die das
Gewissen schnell zum Schweigen bringen
kann. Hinter dieser Stimme aber steht
oft die Faulheit oder der Hochmut. Um
auch der Gut zu sein und nur nach einem
Gewissen zu handeln, daß wir sagt: Die
Erziehung soll deinem Leib bestimmen"
ist das Zweite, was ich brauchen will.

Als letztes hatte ich immer Freiheit und immer Leben genannt. – Unsere Klasse, als der mathematischen Abteilung, wird oft von der sprachlichen Klasse vorgeworfen, wir verstehen ja in Formeln und Berechnungen und sehen an nichts anderes, als an die Mathematik und die einen anderen naturwissenschaftlichen Zweige, und wüßten gar nicht einmal schöner die Sprachen zu... Wir wißten nichts von dem Wert der griechischen Dichter, und ... ja nicht, ... einen guten Gedicht oder ein anderes Werk zu geben ... Jetzt lachen wir noch über solche Vorwürfe, weil wir die anderen Klasse zu ... zu gut kennen und ... wissen, daß ... großen „...

uns gerade auf dem Gebiet, auf dem sie
uns Unbekanntes vornehmen, selbst nicht
viel voraus sind. Heute lachen wir noch
darüber. Was wird aber später sein? Denn
daß das, was man uns jetzt noch im Spaß
und vielleicht unbegründet vorwirft, uns
später wirklich gefangen halten und
blind machen kann, will ich nicht abstrei-
ten. Ich glaube auch, daß gerade wir, deren
Beruf ja später auch wahrscheinlich auf techni-
schem Gebiet liegen wird, besonders leicht dieser
Gefahr erliegen können. Jetzt ist nur die
Frage, inwieweit man von dem Wunsch, in-
nerlich nicht zu erstarren und zu sterben, sich
in der Wahl des Berufes bestimmen lassen
darf, und ob man es überhaupt darf. Hinsicht

Könnte man sich wohl vorstellen, daß jemand,
der an nichts, als an seine Arbeit denkt, und
sich ihr ganz widmet, mehr leisten wird,
wie jemand, der sich auch Zeit nimmt
Bücher zu lesen, und von dem immer
Ringen und Kämpfen der Menschen hören, und der sich auch niemals Gedanken
über Dinge macht, an die ein anderer
nicht denkt, oder nicht denken zu brauchen
glaubt. Andererseits ist der Mensch aber auch
keine Maschine oder Werkzeug, mit dem
sich ... und ... läßt, wie mit
toten Dingen. Oder wird, das zu sein, doch
verlangt, wenn Pflichterfüllung verlangt
wird? Denn der Staat fordert doch alle
Kraft und unseren ganzen Einsatz.

Hat er aber auch das Recht, das von uns
zu fordern, was uns zum Menschen macht? –
Ich kann dir die geheime Hoffnung nicht
nehmen und weiß jetzt noch nicht, wie
ich mich in einem Zweifelsfall, der von
einer kleinen Entscheidung fordern würde, ver-
halten sollte. Im allgemeinen, glaube ich,
wird es aber wohl möglich sein, beides mitein-
ander zu vereinigen, und ich denke die mei-
sten Menschen tun das auch. Denn wer
tut verstohlen seine Pflicht und denkt nicht
auch manchmal an sich. Wer kann denn sagen: „Ich habe in meinem Leben nur meiner
Pflicht gelebt.“? Im Grunde ist der Menschen zu sich immer besser, nur daß jener
sein Leben mehr von der Pflicht, und der

ordnen von seiner Religion und den Über-
zeugungen nach seines Lebens bestimmen
läßt. Es soll mich bei meiner Entscheidung des Lebens hinaus ...,
die solche Arbeit zu ... , die ...
zu einem ... Leben ...
werden. Denn ich will lieber alle die Zweifel
und Sorgen, die sich immer im andern
Falle ... werden, auf mich nehmen
und um ihre Lösung ringen, als ...,
... mir nur ein bloß ... sein.
Dieses sind die drei Gedanken, die mein
Leben bestimmen sollen. Es mag sein, daß
... und ...
... und ... sein. Auch wird
man vielleicht nicht ..., weshalb

ich gerade diese Punkte herausgegriffen habe. Denn sicher werden andere Menschen auch mit anderen Zweifeln zu ringen haben und sich andere Richtlinien nach anderen Gesichtspunkten ziehen. Ich will ja auch nicht sagen, daß meine Anschauung allgemein gültig wäre. Ich glaube sogar selbst, daß ich in einigen Jahren schon über manches anders denken werde, und daß mir auch noch Fragen über Dinge kommen werden, die mir jetzt noch ganz klar und eindeutig erscheinen. Denn ich habe mir vorgenommen, immer bereit zu sein zu lernen und Lehrweis anzunehmen, und wenn ich auch alles, was ich bisher geglaubt habe, aufgeben und als falsch ansehen müßte. Und-

halb soll das, was ich geschrieben habe, nicht
als meine feststehende Anschauung ange-
sehen werden, sondern vielmehr nur als
ein Bild, das meine Zukunft, wie ich sie
jetzt sehe, zeigen soll. Es soll nur einen
Ausschnitt oder ein kleines Stück von dem
Weg wiedergeben, auf dem ich mich bemühe
vorwärts zu kommen, dessen Ende ich aber
noch nicht weiß.

Die Gedanken, die Sie sich über die Wahl
Ihres Berufes machen, zeigen Ihnen, daß
Sie die für Sie im Augenblick wichtigste
Frage mit Verantwortungsbewußtsein und dem
Ernst nicht beten, den diese – meist einmalige –
Entscheidung im Leben wirklich verdient. In
meiner Gedankenschilderung haben Sie auch alles Er-

deutliche Fingerzeige, daß Ihre Entscheidung zu
beeinflussen vermöchte. Ich zweifle niemals
daran, daß Sie später Ihre Wahl gewiß so
noch nehmen wie im Augenblick die Entscheidung zum Wahlergebnis, und dieses Bewußt-
sein ist für einen selber mit das Schönste,
daß ihm das in der Auseinandersetzung mit
seinem Selber begegnen kann. Und noch eine
besondere ernstliche Feststellung: Sie lassen
nicht von der Art, der Sie zugehören.

Sehr gut.

y

Rb. 26. 1. 38.

THE HISTORY OF
THE BERTELSMANN
CORPORATION:
AN OVERVIEW

1835:   The lithographer Carl Bertelsmann founds
            the C. Bertelsmann Publishing House with
            its own printing press—focus is on Christian
            devotional literature.

1850:   Carl Bertelsmann dies and Heinrich
            Bertelsmann takes over the publishing business
            (1827–1887).

1852–87:   Bertelsmann involvement and takeover of
            other German publishing houses (for example,
            Fridrich'scher Verlag 1852, Liesching Verlag
            1861 and 1869, Dümmler Verlag 1887).

1887:   Johannes Mohn, Heinrich Bertelsmann's
            son-in-law, continues the family's publishing
            business in the third generation (1896–1930).

1921:   Johannes Mohn retires and hands over the
            family's publishing business to his son Heinrich
            Mohn (1885–1955). At the time, the publishing
            house has eighty-four employees and a turnover
            of approximately 700,000 reichsmark.

1920s: New distribution channels through church
            clubs make the continuation of the publishing
            house possible throughout inflation and world
            economic crisis.

Toward the end of the 1920s:

            Expansion of the publishing program to
            popular literature (fiction)—at first with
            moderate success.

1934:   Breakthrough and great profits with fiction,
            mainly literature on war experiences. During
            World War II, Bertelsmann becomes the largest
            book supplier of the Deutsche Wehrmacht
            (German military).

1935:   100-year anniversary (150 employees).

1939:   Acquisition of the Rufer Verlag; highest number
            of employees thus far: 440.

1941:   Distribution of religious literature exclusively through the Rufer Verlag (until it closes in 1943).

1944:   Trial due to the involvement of upper-level management in illegal paper trading; sentenced to a fine. The publishing house has to close based on a government order (Reichsschriftumskammer). Allied bombings cause first damage to production buildings.

1945:   On March 13, air raids cause great damage to the publishing buildings in Gütersloh.

1946:   Reinhard Mohn (born 1921) returns from an American prisoner of war camp in Kansas (after being taken prisoner in Tunisia in 1943). The British administration accepts the application for a license to publish books.

1947:   Reinhard Mohn takes over the company when the British administration questions Heinrich Mohn's role during the Third Reich. The buildings in the Eickhoffstraße in Gütersloh are rebuilt.

1950:   The first Bertelsmann Leserring (book club) lays the foundation for the Bertelsmann success—within one year the membership grows to 100,000 individuals, and by 1960 the reading circle counts 2.6 million members.

1952:   Foundation of the Ratgeberverlag and the
           Lexikon Verlag—Bertelsmann becomes the
           number one reference publisher in Germany.

1954:   Foundation of the Rheda publishing company.

1956:   Foundation of the Schallplattenring (Record
           Ring).

1957:   Laying of the foundation stone for the record
           company Sonopress (company begins operation
           in 1958).

1958:   Foundation of Ariola—after initial difficulties
           in the 1960s, the new label celebrates successes
           with national and international singers.

1960:   125-year anniversary.

           Introduction of the Grundsatz- und
           Betriebsordnung (Company Principles,
           precursor to the later Company Constitution):
           The principles are cooperative leadership,
           delegation of responsibility, corporate
           responsibility toward society, and
           decentralization.

1961:   Foundation of the Europaring der Buch- und
           Schallplattenfreunde (European Ring of Book
           and Record Friends).

1962:   First book club abroad: Círculo de Lectores,
           Spain.

1964:   Takeover of the UFA (among other things,
           UFA International and UFA TV productions).
           First Book Center of the book club (today, Club
           Center) opens in Kiel, Germany.

1968:   Reorganization of the company's publishing
           arm—individual publishing houses are
           combined to the Verlagsgruppe Bertelsmann
           GmbH (Bertelsmann Corporation).

1969:   Diversification into the newspaper business
           with an acquisition of a 25 percent share in
           the publishing house Gruner+Jahr (1973: 60
           percent; 1975: 69.9 percent; 1976: 74.9 percent).

1970:   Implementation of capital building and profit
           sharing for employees (starting retroactively on
           April 4, 1969).

           Foundation of the book club France Loisirs
           with the French publisher Presses de la Cité.

           Bertelsmann buys a third of Springer Verlag—
           and sells it shortly thereafter.

           Takeover of the paper factory Cartiere del
           Garda, Italy.

1971:   Transformation of Bertelsmann into a public
           stock company, the Bertelsmann AG—
           Reinhard Mohn becomes first CEO, Gerd

Bucherius becomes first chairman of the board (part owner since the exchange of his ownership of Gruner+Jahr in 1973).

Distinction of five corporate divisions: book and record clubs; publishers; print and industrial companies; music, film, TV; and Gruner+Jahr.

1973:   Implementation of an expanded corporate constitution.

1974:   The foundation stone is laid for the new corporate headquarters in Gütersloh.

1975:   Foundation of Ariola America Inc.—first step into the American market. Sonopress begins production of first music cassettes.

1976:   Takeover of the printing house Tiefdruckerei Belser in Stuttgart, Germany.

Majority investment in maul+co., Nuremberg, Germany.

Move into the new corporate headquarters in Gütersloh.

1977:   Founding of the Bertelsmann Foundation.

Investment in the publishing house Plaza y Janés in Barcelona, Spain. Majority investment in the pocket book publisher Bantam Books in New York, USA (1980: 100 percent ownership)—base for the expansion into the U.S. book market.

First employee questionnaire.

1979:   Takeover of Arista Record Inc. in the United States and in Great Britain.

1981:   Reinhard Mohn moves to the supervisory board; new CEO: Manfred Fischer (until 1983).

Sonopress begins the production of videocassettes.

1983:   Mark Wössner becomes new CEO.

Cooperation with Radio Corporation of America (RCA) in music.

1984:   Involvement in the first German-speaking private TV channel, RTL, and foundation of the UFA-Film und Fernseh-GmbH (UFA Film and TV Company).

Sonopress begins the production of CDs in Gütersloh.

1985:   150-year anniversary—numerous celebrations in the corporate headquarters and the city of Gütersloh.

Foundation of the corporate division for electronic media.

1986:   Introduction of the Bertelsmann-Genusscheine (Bertelsmann Profit Sharing Certificate) at the stock market.

Takeover of the publisher Doubleday and foundation of the Bantam Doubleday Dell Publishing Group.

1987:   Takeover of RCA—combining the music label RCA and Ariola into Bertelsmann Music Group (BMG) with headquarters in New York City.

1989:   First Club Centers open in the new German states (Dresden) in December.

Since 1990: Numerous investments in the new German states, including the creation of the Deutsche Buch-Gemeinschaft (Book and Record Club), supplying investment means (around DM 1 billion).

1991:   Reinhard Mohn retires from active membership on the supervisory board (now only honorary member).

1992:   Purchase of an office building on Broadway in New York City ("Bertelsmann Building").

1993:   Beginning of the private channels VOX
           and RTL 2 (Ufa share about 24.9 percent,
           respectively 7.8 percent).

           Of capital ownership, 68 percent moves
           from Reinhard Mohn to the Bertelsmann
           Foundation.

1994:   Rupert Murdoch invests in VOX (49.9 percent).

1995:   Joint venture between Bertelsmann and
           America Online Inc. as "Canal+Ufa" to
           purchase TV rights.

           Following his death, Gerd Bucherius stock
           transfers to the ZEIT-Foundation.

1996:   America Online (AOL) starts operating in
           Great Britain, France, and Canada.

1997:   Foundation of the first book club in China
           (Shanghai).

           Foundation of the CLT-Ufa in Luxembourg
           by Bertelsmann and Audiofina—this creates
           Europe's largest radio and TV company.

1998:   Takeover of the publisher Random House and
           the foundation of a publishing group with the
           same name as umbrella organization for all
           international book publishing ventures—to

date, the largest investment in the company's history.

Thomas Middelhoff replaces Mark Wössner as CEO (Wössner moves to the supervisory board).

Bertelsmann asks an independent historical commission to research the company's history in the Third Reich.

Implementation of the Bertelsmann Essentials (Responsibility, Objective, Basic Values).

1999:   Reinhard Mohn revises the stockholders' voting rights and transfers his vote to the newly founded Bertelsmann Verwaltungsgesellschaft mbH (BVG).

Expansive restructuring and renaming of all company divisions. For example, the Industrie AG and the service division become the Arvato AG, the Mohn printing group becomes Mohn-Media; the Bertelsmann Book Club in the United States becomes Doubleday Direct; and the Book of the Month Club (Time Inc.) becomes the Joint Venture Bookspan.

2000:   CLT-UFA, Pearson TV, and Audiofina fuse to RTL Group, the largest radio and film corporation in Europe.

RTL Group London goes public.

The exhibition pavilion "Planet M" at the World Expo becomes the first common corporate platform for the Bertelsmann family—the goal is corporate branding (Bertelsmann media worldwide).

Bertelsmann takes the Internet company Lycos public in Europe.

Bertelsmann announces that they will leave the Internet business and sells its shares of AOL Europe for a company record of $6.75 billion to AOL.

2001:   Bertelsmann purchases the majority of the RTL group: Groupe Bruxelles Lambert (GBL) receives 25.1 percent of Bertelsmann stock (0.1 percent without vote) in the Bertelsmann AG in exchange for the GBL shares of RTL.

Bertelsmann takes over the last 50 percent of the French book club France Loisirs from Vivendi Universal Publishing.

2002:   Reinhard Mohn's new provisions strengthen the family's long-term influence at Bertelsmann. Liz Mohn becomes chairwoman of the shareholder association and general manager of the Bertelsmann Verwaltungsgesellschaft; the

BVG holds 100 percent of the vote in the main assembly of the Bertelsmann AG.

Gunter Thielen becomes new CEO—Thomas Middelhoff leaves the company.

Bertelsmann takes over the Pearson Media corporation's shares of the RTL Group.

The DirectGroup Bertelsmann sells the Internet-bookseller BOL.

BMG takes over Zomba Music Group—BMG already bought 25 percent in 1991 and 20 percent more in 1996 of Zomba Publishing and Zomba Music.

The independent historical commission presents its final report on "Bertelsmann in the Third Reich" in book form.

2003:   On November 6, Bertelsmann AG and Bertelsmann Foundation open the Bertelsmann Building in Berlin, Germany. The address "Unter den Linden 1" (UDL) becomes synonymous for the corporation's presence in the German capital.

Random House Germany takes over the Heyne Verlag from Springer and thus a number of internationally successful authors.

          Finalizing the repurchase of stock from the ZEIT-Foundation.

2004:   Bertelsmann Music Group fuses with Sony Music to SonyBMG and becomes the third-largest music distributor in the world.

          The RTL Group sells its shares of the international sports management group Sportfive.

2005:   DirectGroup Bertelsmann takes over Columbia House, the largest U.S. distributor for DVDs.

          Beginning of the GAIN initiative (Growth and Innovation) to signal new corporate investments.

          "You are Germany" campaign—well-respected call for social responsibility and unity.

2006:   Repurchasing of all shares of the GBL for 4.5 billion euros—for the first time since 1973, there is no other shareholder at the Bertelsmann Corporation (76.9 percent is held by the Bertelsmann Foundation, 23.1 percent by the Mohn family).

          Opening of a Bertelsmann branch in China (Beijing).

          New version of the Essentials.

2007:   Closing of the Napster trials—legal
            disagreements with several music distributors
            ends after settlement payments by Bertelsmann.

2008:   January 1, Hartmut Ostrowski becomes
            new CEO—Gunter Thielen moves to the
            supervisory board of the Bertelsmann
            Foundation.

Special thanks to Helen Müller and her team at the Bertelsmann Corporate Archives.

NOTES

FAMILY ORIGINS AND PERSONAL LESSONS

1. Plato provides the connection between this statement and the pre-Socratic thinker Heraclites, by summarizing and interpreting the Herclitean philosophy as constant flow/river/change: *"Pánta choreì kaì oudèn ménei,"* "everything moves and nothing remains the same." The philosophy of Heraclites has survived only in fragments. Compare Wilhelm Capelle, *Die Vorsokratiker, Fragmente und Qellenberichte,* Stuttgart: 1968.

2. Compare the homework essay Reinhard Mohn, Private Archive, translation and facsimile here on pages 135–166.

3. The report of an independent group of historians under the direction of historian Saul Friedländer provided a detailed historical reappraisal of the history of the Bertelsmann publishing house in the years between 1933 and 1945. Compare *Bertelsmann im Dritten Reich,* München: Bertelsmann, 2002.

4. Compare Reinhard Mohn, *Der direkte Weg zum Leser: "Die Königsidee Buchgemeinschaft,"* draft of a speech from January 9, 1985. Bertelsmann Corporate Archives.

5. Compare *Bertelsmann im Dritten Reich,* pp. 515ff.

6. *An meine Mitarbeiter. Eine Ansprache zum Jahreswechsel 1946/47.* Bertelsmann Corporate Archives.

7. Compare Reinhard Mohn, *Der direkte Weg zum Leser.*

8. Ibid.

9. *Tagebuch Rudolf Wendorff,* March 17, 1946.

EXPERIENCES OF AN ENTREPRENEUR

1. Conversations with Andrea Stoll and Jochen Werner, January 11, 2008.

2. My source of inspiration in those years was the discovery of the American author and management consultant Peter Drucker. Compare Peter Drucker, *Praxis des Managements. Ein Leitfaden für die Führungs-Aufgaben in der modernen Wirtschaft,* Düsseldorf: Econ, 1998.

3. Compare *Betriebsordnung der Firmen C. Bertelsmann Verlag, Bertelsmann GmbH, Ariola GmbH, Verlagsgemeinschaft Bertelsmann GmbH, Vertriebsgemeinschaft Buch und Wissen GmbH* from January 10, 1956. Bertelsmann Corporate Archives, 3rd Edition, March 1, 1959, p. 2.

4. Despite intensive research, the exact time frame of these incidents can no longer be reconstructed.

5. *Grundsatzordnung und Betriebsordnung für die Firmen des Hauses Bertelsmann.* Gütersloh, September 1, 1960. Bertelsmann Corporate Archives.

6. Ibid.

7. Ibid.

8. Reading Klaus Mehnert's *Asien, Moskau und wir* (Stuttgart: Deutsche Verlags-Anstalt, 1956) was extremely helpful.

9. *Reisebericht Reinhard Mohn, Moskau-Reise 1957.* Bertelsmann Corporate Archives.

10. Ibid.

11. Ibid.

12. In addition to classics such as Dostoyevsky, Tolstoy, and Pasternak, we added the authors Antonia Koptjajeva, Vladimir Dudinzev, Mikhail Scholokhov, and Stalin's daughter Svetlana Allilujeva to the publishing program of the Sigbert Mohn publishing house and the reading circle.

13. The literary rank and great popularity of Spanish writing authors such as Octavio Paz, José Saramago, Camilo José Cela, Mario Vargas Llosa, Rafael Alberti, and Carlos Fuentes had an enormous influence on Spanish cultural life.

14. Reinhard Mohn, *Der direkte Weg zum Leser*: "Die Königsidee Buchgemeinschaft," draft of a speech from January 9, 1985. Bertelsmann Corporate Archives.

15. Compare mainly Reinhard Mohn, "Moderne Führungstechnik und ihre gesellschaftspolitischen Konsequenzen" in *Zeitschrift für betriebswirtschaftliche Forschung, hg. im Auftrag der Schmalenbach-Gesellschaft,* Sonderheft 1, 1972, manuscript undated. Bertelsmann Corporate Archives. Compare also Reinhard Mohn, *Erfolg durch Partnerschaft. Eine Unternehmensstrategie für den Menschen,* Berlin: Seidler, 1986.

16. Conversations with Andrea Stoll and Willi Pfannkuche, January 30, 2008.

17. *Briefwechsel Reinhard Mohn* 1967–1969. Bertelsmann Corporate Archives.

18. Ibid.

19. Compare Reinhard Mohn, *Erfolg durch Partnerschaft,* Berlin: Siedler, 1986.

20. This assessment has been confirmed by many important economic leaders. Regarding the current debate, compare Alan Greenspan, *Mein Leben für die Wirtschaft,* Frankfurt/New York: Auflage, 2007, p. 31.

21. Compare Tony Judt, *Europa von 1945 bis zur Gegenwart,* Munich: Hanser, 2006.

22. Compare ibid., pp. 399ff.

23. Compare Jürgen Eick, "Hin zur parasitären Gesellschaft?" in *Frankfurter Allgemeine Zeitung,* October 7, 1981.

24. Compare Reinhard Mohn, *Demokratie in Staat und Wirtschaft: Plädoyer für eine Neugestaltung unseres Gesellschaftssystems. Referat vor der Europäischen Bildungsgemeinschaft,* Stuttgart, March 18, 1974. Bertelsmann Corporate Archives.

25. Compare Reinhard Mohn, *Die gesellschaftliche Verantwortung des Unternehmers,* Munich, 2003.

26. Compare *Diskussion zwischen Reinhard Mohn und dem DGB-Vorsitzenden Heinz Oskar Vetter im Kaisershof in Gütersloh,* Westfalenblatt, February 1974. Gütersloh City Archives.

27. Compare Stefano Carboni, *Venice and the Islamic World, 828–1797,* New Haven: Yale University Press, 2007.

28. Compare the culture historical analysis of author Ilija Trojanow and Ranjit Hoskoté, *Kampfabsage: Cultures Do Not Fight Each*

Other, They Flow into Each Other/Together/Combine, Munich: Blessing, 2007.

29. Compare "Georg Wilhelm Friedrich Hegel, *Philosophie des Rechts, 1920*" in Georg Hegel and Gesammelte Werke, eds., *Eva Moldenhauer und Karl Markus Michel,* vol. 7, Frankfurt 1970, pp. 503–512, and "Philosophie der Geschichte, 1821" in *Eva Moldenhauer,* vol. 12, pp. 97–105.

30. "Essai sur les mœurs et l'esprit des nations," *Œuvres Complètes de Voltaire,* vol. 16, Paris 1784, p. 241.

31. Compare Reinhard Mohn, "Die neuen Aufgaben heißen Führung und Geleit" in *Frankfurter Allgemeine Zeitung,* October 8, 2005.

32. Compare the large publishing program of the Bertelsmann Foundation: www.bertelsmann-stiftung.de/verlag.

33. Compare Kwame Anthony Appiah, *Der Kosmopolit: Philosophie des Weltbürgertums,* Munich: Auflage, 2007.

ON THE ROAD INTO THE FUTURE

1. Compare Reinhard Mohn, *Erfolg durch Partnerschaft* and Reinhard Mohn, *Menschlichkeit gewinnt. Ein Bericht an den Club of Rome,* Gütersloh: Bertelsmann Stiftung, 2000. Compare Reinhard Mohn, *Die gesellschaftliche Verantwortung des Unternehmers.*

2. Compare Victor Hugo, *Eröffnungsrede zum Pariser Friedenskongress,* August 21, 1849.

3. Compare the cultural analysis of Samuel P. Huntington, *Kampf der Kulturen: Die Neugestaltung der Weltpolitik im 21. Jahrhundert,* Munich: Goldmann, 1996.

4. Ibid.

5. Compare Reinhard Mohn, "Demokratie und Führung als Zukunftsaufgaben" in *Frankfurter Allgemeine Zeitung,* May 6, 2006.

6. Compare Huntington, *Kampf der Kulturen.*

7. Compare Walter Bröcker, ed., *Platons Gespräche,* Frankfurt, 1967.

8. Compare Bertelsmann Stiftung, ed., *Religionsmonitor 2008,* Gütersloh, 2007.

9. Compare Walter Kardinal Kasper, "Ein Blick über Europa hinaus" in *Religionsmonitor,* p. 140.

10. With regard to the current debate, compare Heinz-Joachim Fischer, "Ziel des Dialogs: Was noch fehlt im Gespräch zwischen Christen und Muslimen" in *Frankfurter Allgemeine Zeitung*, May 14, 2008.

11. Marc Aurel, *Selbstbetrachtungen* IX, 5.

12. Compare Erfolg durch Partnerschaft, *Analyseergebnisse zum Zusammenhang zwischen Unternehmenskultur und wirtschaftlichem Erfolg*, Gütersloh: 2008.

INDEX OF NAMES

ABOUT THE AUTHORS

Reinhard Mohn, born in Gütersloh, Germany, in 1921, is the great-grandson of Bertelsmann's founding publisher, Carl Bertelsmann. In five decades under his leadership, Bertelsmann grew to be one of the world's leading media conglomerates. He is married to Liz Mohn and has six children.

Andrea Stoll, Ph.D., studied German, philosophy, and journalism in Mainz and Vienna. Since 1992 she has worked as a freelance writer and producer for book publishers, film studios, and television stations and as a lecturer at the University of Salzburg. She has published numerous essays and several books, specializing in biographic and socio-political topics.